To me, humor was the best part of baseball. Most of the recent baseball books, I realized, concentrated on statistics. The dry stuff. There are books that will tell you which left-handed batter does the best against left-handed pitchers in the ninth inning of one-run games. There are books that will tell you when to throw a curveball in the dirt to Bo Jackson. And there are books that will tell you who is the best designated hitter on artificial turf. Finally, there is this book, which will tell you absolutely none of that.

I thought it would be fun to put together a different kind of baseball book, a collection of all the funny, unusual, odd things that take place during a typical baseball season. So at the beginning of the 1989 baseball season I started collecting all of the funny lines and unusual plays and odd events that took place. And that's what this book is all about. A lot of unpleasant things took place in the baseball world in 1989, and I'm not going to write about them. I'm going to focus on the good parts. Other people may want to write about them. I don't. Not one word. Not one syllable.

Okay, maybe I will write about some of these things. But only the funny parts.

Bantam Books of Related Interest

Ask your bookseller for the books you have missed

BASEBALL LITE

Ron Luciano
with
David Fisher

BANTAM BOOKS
NEW YORK • TORONTO • LONDON • SYDNEY • AUCKLAND

BASEBALL LITE

A Bantam Book / April 1990

Grateful acknowledgment is made for permission to reprint excerpts from the following: "Ramblin Rose" by Joe Sherman and Nat Sherman, © 1962, renewed 1990 by Sweco Music Corporation. All rights controlled and administered by EMI Blackwood Music Inc. Under license from ATV Music (Sweco), "When Will I Be Loved" by Phil Everly, © 1960, renewed 1988 Acuff-Rose Music, Inc. All rights reserved. International copyright secured. Used by permission. Grateful acknowledgment is also made to Bob Sheppard for permission to use the poem appearing on page 151.

Designed and produced by M 'N O Production Services, Inc.

ISBN 0-553-28447-9

Published simultaneously in the United States and Canada

Bantam Books are published by Bantam Books, a division of Bantam Doubleday Dell Publishing Group, Inc. Its trademark, consisting of the words "Bantam Books" and the portrayal of a rooster, is Registered in U. S. Patent and Trademark Office and in other countries. Marca Registrada, Bantam Books, 666 Fifth Avenue, New York, New York 10103

PRINTED IN THE UNITED STATES OF AMERICA

0 9 8 7 6 5 4 3 2 1

The authors would like to gratefully dedicate this book to the brilliant people who had the foresight and humor to purchase it; and we would specifically not dedicate this book to those less brilliant people who are reading somebody else's copy.

The authors would like to acknowledge the assistance of the following people, without whose efforts this book could never have been completed: At Bantam Books—Lou Aronica, Tom Dyja, Bev Susswein, Matt Shear, and Julia Marson; Michael Mendelsohn and Pat Ollague of M 'N O Production Services; Alan Bruns; the Cleon Montgomery family; Frank Biondo; Bob DiNunzio; the Jester family—Dee, Jonathan, Brian, Kevin, and Jane; the Walton Family—Barbara, Richard, and Kevin, as well as newcomers Burke and Jason; the inimitable Tedd Webb, Jay Redick, Patricia Brown, and John Boswell; and the beautiful Nell Rogers for her perfect paper collecting.

"What managing a club does for you is make you feel alive. Day to day you're happy, you're depressed...you work in an atmosphere of genuine excitement. The laughs are a major feature. The games are tense and those playing in them are serious, but throughout the whole clubhouse there is always an undertow of laughter. Guys are always doing something, or saying something, that makes the others laugh. Even when people are long out of baseball, they remember the laughs."

—CALIFORNIA ANGELS MANAGER DOUG RADER

"When you're done, you only tell your grandchildren about the good things. If they ask me about 1989, I'll tell them I had amnesia."

—DETROIT TIGERS MANAGER SPARKY ANDERSON

BASEBALL
LITE

It's not my fault.

My name is Ron Luciano with David Fisher. When I was growing up in Endicott, New York, my parents taught me that when I failed I had to try, try again. And as anyone who knows me will admit, I'm a very trying person. And I'm going to keep trying. The truth is that the thing I've been most successful at in my life is failing. When it comes to failing, I'm a very big success. It seems that wherever I go, failure seems to follow. Let me put it this way: vampires wear garlic around their neck to keep me away.

The year *after* I was an All-American football player at Syracuse University, for example, the Orange won the national championship. When the Detroit Lions drafted me they were among pro football's dominant teams. Remember the Detroit Lions? Then I was signed by the Buffalo Bills, one of the best teams in the American Football League. Remember the American Football League? I spent four years in pro football without ever playing in a single regular-season game. After finishing my football career I became a math teacher. Everybody knows what has happened to the entire American educational system. So I decided to become a baseball umpire, starting in the

D leagues, the lowest classification. You'll notice there no longer are D leagues. Or C leagues or B leagues. I finally made it to the major leagues as an American League umpire in 1968. Only twelve years later the American League won another All-Star Game. In 1980 NBC hired me as an announcer on Baseball's Game of the Week— and major league baseball immediately went on strike. NBC had also paid hundreds of millions of dollars for the rights to broadcast the Olympics. The American team didn't participate. Finally, I left NBC and opened a sporting goods store. In my case it turned out to be a sporting bads store. I put an entire mall out of business. Then I started doing commercials on network television—cable immediately got very big. I became the spokesperson for Gulf Oil of Canada. They sold the company and changed the name. Fortunately, they still call the country Canada. So far.

Some people seem to have a black cloud hovering over their heads. I've got the hole in the ozone layer.

After being out of baseball for a few years I found that the thing I missed most of all was the good humor on the field. The players and managers were always saying funny things to me like, "Move around, Luciano, you're killing the grass," "I've seen better calls at a hog fair," "With a face like yours, no wonder they make you wear a mask," "I heard you ate everything on the menu last night, including the squashed flies," "That's only your shadow? I thought it was a total eclipse," "You're not supposed to make long distance calls." And, of course, the great one: "Maybe you're not the worst umpire in the entire history of baseball, but I've only been in baseball thirty years." We sure had some good laughs on the field.

And I missed it. To me, that humor was the best part of baseball. Most of the recent baseball books, I realized, concentrated on statistics. The dry stuff. There are books that will tell you which left-handed batter does the best against left-handed pitchers in the ninth inning of one-run games. There are books that will tell you when to throw a curveball in the dirt to Bo Jackson. And there are books that will tell you who is the best designated hitter on artificial turf. Finally, there is this book, which will tell you absolutely none of that.

I'm not very good at statistics. I don't even know how much I weigh. When I was teaching math I couldn't even figure out how many kids I had in my classes. But I can tell you that when pitcher Bob Forsch was being measured for his Astro uniform, he was asked how long he wanted his pants, and replied, "For the whole season, I hope." And I can tell you that Mets broadcaster Ralph Kiner informed his listeners that pitcher Bruce Sutter had reinjured his arm and, according to Kiner, "He's probably going to be out of action for the rest of his career." And I can tell you that pitcher Larry Andersen wondered, "Why is it that we park in the driveway and drive on the parkway?" And it was Andersen who asked, "Why is it always raining cats and dogs? Why doesn't it ever rain yaks and wildebeests?" Of course, I can't tell you why he asks these things.

Let other people write about line drives, I'm more interested in one-liners. I thought it would be fun to put together a different kind of baseball book, a collection of all the funny, unusual, odd things that take place during a typical baseball season. I wasn't interested in runs, I was looking for puns. So at the beginning of the 1989 baseball season I started collecting all of the funny lines and unusual plays and odd events that took place.

Naturally I started in 1989. Some funny season. Long before an umpire threw out the first manager it was revealed that Wade Boggs had been having a long-term affair with a woman named Margo Adams. And that Steve

Garvey had impregnated two women, then married a third one. Then Pete Rose was accused of betting on baseball games, and not paying income taxes on certain winnings, and was finally banned from baseball. Nineteen eighty-nine was the year that both baseball commissioner, A. Bartlett Giamatti and Billy Martin died tragically. And Yankee outfielder Luis Polonia was arrested for having sexual relations with a minor. And former Angels relief pitcher Donnie Moore committed suicide. And Jose Canseco was arrested for carrying a gun and received several speeding tickets and finally set up a telephone gimmick that charged callers two dollars to find out what he'd eaten for breakfast. Dave Winfield had a back operation and missed the entire season, then lost a million-dollar paternity suit. In spring training Darryl Strawberry walked out of camp because the Mets wouldn't extend his contract, then returned to get in a fight with Keith Hernandez, and was named in a paternity suit. And finally, the 1989 season will be remembered forever as the year the Bay Bridge World Series between the San Francisco Giants and the Oakland A's was overwhelmed by a devastating earthquake that knocked down a portion of the Bay Bridge.

Meanwhile, I was busy collecting all the funny stuff.

And that's what this book is all about. A lot of unpleasant things took place in the baseball world in 1989, and I'm not going to write about them. I'm going to focus on the good parts. Other people may want to write about them. I don't. Not one word. Not one syllable. I'm not even going to mention that when Tommy Lasorda heard about Steve Garvey's blessed events he asked, "What's he trying to do, become the father of our country?" Or that Wade Boggs said he preferred to think of his mistress, not as his lover, but as his buddy, someone "you could take to a boat show."

Okay, maybe I will write about some of these things. But only the funny parts.

Like every other baseball season, 1989 began with optimism and predictions. And as in every other season, most of the predictions were wrong. For example:

Mets manager Davey Johnson admitted, "There's no question we should be picked to win. We should dominate." After the Mets struggled through the first half of the season, he added, "When we win it, it'll be my most satisfying year in New York."

The Mets finished second, six games behind the Cubs.

Once again, The George Steinbrenner Award for Predicting He Isn't Going to Fire His Manager Award goes to. . . George Steinbrenner. There is a reason the award is named after him. The Boss said at the beginning of the year, "I will bet you [Dallas Green] will be there at the end of the World Series when we win it...Dallas has no problems this year at all." A month later he insisted, "Dallas Green will continue to manage the team this year, no matter what...I know some people will say it's usually the kiss of death from me, but it isn't." In July he added, "If you're asking me, 'Are there going to be any managerial changes?' the answer is no." And in August he repeated, "I'm still supportive of my manager and have no plans to replace him."

Green was fired in August and replaced by Bucky Dent.

Green was probably not surprised. In the spring, after being told about the Boss's statements, he asked, "If I go 1–161, I'm still here?"

In the category of Worst Prediction of the Year, Managers, the winner is Toronto Blue Jays Manager Cito Gaston. When the Blue Jays fired manager Jimy Williams,

Gaston agreed to take the job on an interim basis, only until a permanent replacement could be hired. "I could never manage this team," he explained, "I'm too close to the players."

Named permanent manager after Steinbrenner refused to release Lou Piniella from his Yankee contract, Gaston led Toronto to the Eastern Division title.

In the Worst Prediction of the Year, Players, Category, the winner is the Mets' Darryl Strawberry. During the spring he vowed, "I'm going to have a monster year this year and another one next year. I'm dedicated, totally committed...I may hit fifty homers this year. I'm going to have an awesome year. A monster season... This year I'm going to amaze a lot of people. I'll probably even amaze the front office..."

Sometimes you get the monster, and sometimes the monster gets you. The Straw Man was partially right— his season was monstrous. He hit a career-low .225 with only 77 RBIs and 29 home runs.

The Most Conservative Prediction of the Year was made, naturally, by President George Bush. Asked in early October who he thought was going to win the American League Eastern Division title, Bush declared firmly, "I've given up on the Rangers."

And people still say this man isn't willing to take chances.

From almost the first day of spring training, Yankee manager Dallas Green suspected it was going to be a long season. After the Yankees' first intrasquad game, played between coach Frank Howard's "Jumbo Franks" and coach Pat Corrales's "O.K. Corrales," Green complained that the team had missed the cutoff man, missed signs, failed to convert hit-and-run opportunities, failed to advance runners, failed to score runners from third base with less than two out, and had two players injured.

But other than that, Dallas, how was the ball game?

That turned out to be a pretty accurate omen. During the season the Yankees had fifty different players on their roster, the most on any team since the 1969 expansion Seattle Pilots. This inspired Rafael Santana to suggest in mid-season, "We'll have to take the team picture every day from now through October 2."

The Yankee situation got so bad that Don Mattingly suggested, "It's like being in the middle of the kitchen when your wife is having a tirade... Maybe it's time to grow our hair long, wear earrings, wear jeans on the plane, and turn ourselves into the Oakland Raiders of baseball."

The Yankees were not the only team to disappoint their fans. The Pirates had been expected to contend for the National League East title, but fell apart. They ranked last in defense in the National League, causing outfielder Andy Van Slyke to admit, "They had better defense at Pearl Harbor."

After ending the season with a loss to the Mets, Pittsburgh manager Jim Leyland summed up the season accurately: "This is a blah ending to a blah season."

The Detroit Tigers were so bad offensively that they even lost an exhibition game to their Triple A affiliate, the Toledo Mud Hens. In that game they were shut out on three hits for five innings by forty-year-old John Wockenfuss, a former catcher now managing Toledo. "It's been a Murphy's Law season for us," pitcher Doyle Alexander said. "Whatever can go wrong has... 'Frustration' is no longer the word. 'Pathetic' is a better word."

Few teams had a more disappointing season than the Montreal Expos. After trading three young pitchers to Seattle for Mark Langston, the Expos were in first place in August. "I consider us to be the team to beat," manager Buck Rodgers said. "I think everybody else does, too. We're not looking back..."

Tim Raines was looking in another direction. He summed up the Expos' problems by pointing out, "I can see a hundred guys left on third base."

The most surprising teams of the 1989 season were the NL Eastern Division champion Chicago Cubs and the Baltimore Orioles, who finished second in the AL East. Before the season opened, Cardinals manager Whitey Herzog, a master of inside baseball, revealed, "The only way you can beat the Mets is to win more games than they do. I don't know if anybody can do that."

Absolutely no one anticipated the Cubs being the team to do that. "When we broke training camp," Don Zimmer said, "[general manager] Jim Frey and I sat down and both of us agreed that if we could wind up 81–81, we'd go out and celebrate."

Former Cubs catcher Jody Davis was a little more blunt in his appraisal of the Cubs' chances, saying, "They have the potential to be very, very bad."

Even after the Cubs got off to a great start, few players believed they were serious contenders. In June former Cub relief pitcher Frank DiPino, who had been traded to the Cardinals the previous winter, explained why the Cubs were winning. "They've got new faces over there, and the guys just don't know the hitters. Let's see how well they do the second time around...against these teams."

The fact that they stayed in contention through July still didn't change too many opinions. "Bad as we've been," the Pirates' Andy Van Slyke said, "it's not August yet and the Cubs are still in first place."

When they were still in first place in August, a reporter asked Zimmer for an explanation. "If you ask me what's going on here," Zimmer admitted, "all I can say is I have no idea."

The Cubs were still leading the league in September, but Frank DiPino wasn't convinced. "We're going to count on the little bald-headed guy [Zimmer] to mess up," he said. "I think he's doing a good job of it."

And finally, after the Cubs had clinched the division title, Zimmer responded, "All I can say is have a nice winter, Frank. And I'm all out of playoff tickets."

When Cubs star reliever Mitch Williams was asked if he thought 1989 had been a storybook season, he paused, then decided, "I don't know. I didn't read storybooks when I was growing up."

The Orioles won 34 more games in '89 than they had a season earlier, becoming one of only six teams since 1900 to raise their winning percentage more than 200 percentage points in a season. "I can't believe the first place Orioles," Dave Winfield said in June; "it must be their new uniforms."

After leading the league for 97 days, the O's finished second to Toronto. "In 1982 in San Francisco," manager Frank Robinson said, "we finished two games out and they gave me twenty-four hours to get out of town. Here we finish two games out and we get a parade."

The Semi-Sweet
Smell of Success

Without question, there was a Word of the Year. I'm proud to award the first ever Where Have You Gone, Eddie Stanky? Award to the most used word in 1989—"stink."

"Stink" made its first appearance of the season after the Yankees' first loss, when manager Dallas Green said, "They just kicked the hell out of us. It stank."

After losing four in a row, Green amended that to "We stink."

That assessment did not bother owner Steinbrenner. "I love it when the manager says, 'We stink,' or, 'It's my fault.' We haven't had managers be stand-up like that..." Eventually he explained, "He said they stink because they do stink."

Obviously Steinbrenner loved the word so much, he used it himself, telling reporters a few games later, "Our relief pitching stinks right now."

Finally the entire team agreed, serenading Green on a road trip by singing, to the tune of "The Mickey Mouse Club Song," "W-e-d-o-s-t-i-n-k," then adding the chorus, "We do stink, we do stink."

The Yankees were not the only team to stink this year. "We're finding different ways of losing right now,"

Expos manager Buck Rodgers said. "Right now we stink. We stink."

Speaking about the Mets, Darryl Strawberry claimed, "We stink. It's as simple as that."

Pirates manager Jim Leyland had his own opinion. "We stunk."

Tigers pitcher Frank Tanana added a more grammatical "We've stunk."

"My guys didn't pitch too well," Phillies manager Nick Leyva admitted. "In fact, they stunk."

The Blue Jays weren't any better. "We stunk up the place," admitted third baseman Kelly Gruber.

The Mets' Kevin Elster was more specific, saying after a game, "The way we lost stinks."

Tiger manager Sparky Anderson spoke for the entire American League East when claiming, "The Orioles can win because everybody else has stunk up the joint."

Some stinks are more personal than others. "Maybe we do stink," the Pirates' Andy Van Slyke agreed with Leyland. "I know I do."

Mitch Williams felt the same way. "The bullpen has stunk," he said, "and I've been the lead stinker."

"No excuse," the Rangers' Charlie Hough said after a loss. "I just stink."

After making an error, Yankee outfielder Bob Brower admitted, "I just stunk today."

When Braves reliever Joe Boever blew his third consecutive save opportunity, he pointed out, "I'm in a streak of stink."

Making a second appearance in this category is Darryl Strawberry, this time speaking for himself. "I'm having a stink year," he said, "Some people might say stinky." Not on this particular list, however.

After being struck out by Oriole pitcher Jeff

Ballard, Don Mattingly said disgustedly, "I just stunk, really."

There were some people who didn't like it, the Mets' Kevin McReynolds, for example. "It's annoying to have little kids holler at me, 'You're fat and you stink.'"

After Frank Robinson had threatened to quit because he felt the umpires were against him, several close calls went for the Orioles and against California, prompting Angels manager Doug Rader to declare, "It stinks."

The foreign contribution comes from Cubs instructor Jimmy Piersall, who once hosted a radio talk show. "Did you ever try to talk to a football coach or a basketball coach?" he asked. "They're the most boring people on earth...I think sports talk shows are el stinko."

Jose Canseco's anger was directed at the Arizona police officers who stopped his car and issued four tickets. "Their attitude stunk," he said.

Kevin Elster appears in this category for a second time, to give his opinion of the manufacturer of the glove he used to set a record by playing 87 straight games at shortstop without making an error. When they failed to offer him an endorsement contract, he said, "Their management isn't run well. It really stinks."

The old-timer contribution comes from former Chicago Cubs pitcher Bill Hands, who explained how the Cubs blew the 1969 pennant to the Mets. "We didn't play very well down the stretch. In fact, we stunk."

The future-stink contribution comes from Phillie Lenny Dykstra, who promised, "I'm going to sign a one-year deal this winter, and if I go out next year and stink, they can do whatever they want to."

The football contribution comes from Bears coach Mike Ditka, who said after Chicago had dropped an August game to the Kansas City Chiefs, "We absolutely stunk."

And finally, the close-but-no-cigar-smell contribution comes from Darryl Strawberry, whose effort to appear here three times came very close with, "From the start of the season, I'd characterize it as we suck. That's what it boils down to. We suck."

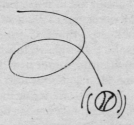

The Kruk of the Matter

Among baseball's most quotable characters is the Philadelphia Phillies' John Kruk. Kruk had had a very tough season in 1988. His batting average had fallen 72 points from '87, the biggest decline in the major leagues, and an old friend who came to stay with him turned out to be a bank robber on the run from the FBI. "My career so far isn't much to brag about," he admitted in spring training. "I've only been in the league three years and I'm already up for the Comeback of the Year Award."

Kruk opened the season with the San Diego Padres in a long batting slump, which he blaimed on the fact that "I forgot to send back a chain letter I got."

When he finally managed to get two hits in one game, a reporter asked him about his state of mind. "I haven't killed myself yet," he said. "I'm pretty proud of that."

Eventually the Padres traded him to the Phillies, and he started hitting again. "The difference was being traded," he claimed. "I came over here and got a chance to play every day. I'm not saying anything bad about

[Padres manager] Jack McKeon. If I was manager, I wouldn't have played me either."

Kruk has some unique theories about hitting. When Phillies batting coach John Vukovich told him he needed to adjust his mechanics, Kruk replied, "The only mechanics I know about are at a gas station."

The fact is that Kruk is not really a student of hitting. "I thought I was hitting Mike LaCoss real good. They they told me I was 0 for 15 against him lifetime."

And he isn't really a student of fielding either. Playing left field against the Pirates, he thought there were two outs, so when R. J. Reynolds hit a routine fly ball to him, he caught it—then held on to it and watched base runner Bobby Bonilla tag up at second and come all the way around to score. "You call that a gastric disturbance of the brain area," he told reporters. "Then I led off the inning. How many times do you see a guy make a great defensive play and lead off the next inning? I'm just glad they don't allow guns in the stadium. I wasn't worried about my career. I was worried about my life."

Finally, when the Phillies got Lenny Dykstra from the Mets in a deal, Kruk was thrilled. "This is like a movie over here now," he said: "Psycho and Psycho II."

The "I Know I Can Manage, I'm Just Not Sure I Can Cope" Department

When a sportswriter asked Mookie Wilson if he'd like to manage when his playing career ended, the Mookster thought about it for a moment, then decided, "Only if they told me I had one year to live."

Managers are like swinging doors: they come, they go, they come, they go, they... When the Blue Jays announced that Cito Gaston was going to be their interim manager, Toronto pitcher Mike Flanagan asked, correctly, "Aren't all managers interim?"

A lot of people think the importance of a manager is overrated. For example, on May 1, Pete Rose's Cincinnati team beat the Expos, 19–6. That was the most runs ever scored against the Expos. The Reds had 21 hits, the most hits they'd had in a decade. And they did it all while manager Rose stayed in his hotel room, suffering from the flu.

This was actually a pretty good year for managers. Only Jimy Williams in Toronto, Dallas Green in New York, and Doc Edwards in Cleveland were fired, while Rose was banned from baseball. That's only 16⅔ percent, an unusually low figure. The Managers of the Year were Don Zimmer in the National League and Frank Robinson in the American League. The biggest news in managing was that, for the first time, baseball had two black managers, Robinson and Cito Gaston, and they met in the American League playoffs. For the record, the first major league game between teams both managed by black men was played on June 27. Blue Jay pitchers walked 15 Oriole batters, and Toronto made 4 errors as Baltimore won, 16-6.

I Think, Therefore
I Am a Manager

One of the most interesting managerial moves of the season was made by Milwaukee Brewers manager Tom Trebelhorn. In the ninth inning of a game against Toronto, right-handed reliever Chuck Crim was on the mound. When switch-hitter Nelson Liriano came to bat, Trebelhorn brought in left-handed reliever Tony Fossas to force Liriano to hit right-handed. But instead of taking out Crim, he moved him to first base. "I wondered," Crim said later, "if they hit the ball to me, what in the world am I going to do?" Liriano singled. Trebelhorn took out Fossas, returned Crim to the mound, and inserted first baseman Terry Francona. Crim retired the next two batters to save the game. Afterward Trebelhorn explained what had happened. "I think the best way to sum it up is that Chuck Crim relieved himself on the mound in front of 40,000 people."

A good candidate for the worst bit of managerial strategy has to be the decision made by Boston Red Sox manager Joe Morgan in the eleventh inning of a game against the Yankees. With two out, the Yankees had the winning run on second. Right-handed reliever Bob Stanley was on the mound, and left-hand hitting rookie "Neon" Deion Sanders was batting for New York. Sanders, playing in only his seventh major league game, after less than a full season in the low minors, was batting only .154. On deck for the Yanks was their right-handed hitting All-Star second baseman, Steve Sax, who was batting .307. Morgan ordered Stanley to walk Sanders and pitch to Sax. Sax lined Stanley's second pitch into center field to win the ball game. Sanders probably summed up the prevailing opinion, admitting, "I sure wouldn't have walked me."

Morgan actually had a tough year. At one point during the season he surprised a lot of people by starting his right-handed-hitting catcher, Rick Cerone, against right-handed pitcher Shawn Hillegas, instead of left-handed-hitting catcher Rich Gedman. When reporters asked him why he'd started Cerone, Morgan gave them the obvious answer: "I thought Hillegas was a lefty."

Morgan has always been very honest. After Sam Horn went 0 for 18 as a pinch-hitter, Morgan decided to start him in a few games. "I know he can't pinch-hit," he explained, "but I don't hold that against him. I couldn't either."

When Bob Stanley publicly criticized some of Morgan's decisions, Morgan refused to respond. "I don't bury guys," he said. "I let Hebner do that." In the off-season, coach Richie Hebner has dug graves in a cemetery owned by his father.

The biggest problem Morgan had to deal with in 1989 was the Boggs—Margo Adams scandal. But he faced it head on. When a caller to his weekly television show asked him about it, he replied, "Boy, that little Michael Adams [of Boston College] is a hell of a basketball player, isn't he?"

The Boys of Zimmer

ZimBall, as played by the Cubs this year, consisted of hitting-and-running with the bases loaded, suicide squeeze bunts, bunting with two strikes, and stealing bases in unusual situations. "Don Zimmer isn't the manager of the year," one writer decided. "He's the manager of the century."

The Cubs were 50 to 1 to win the division title at the beginning of the year. The team was awful in spring training. Five years ago, when Cubs general manager Jim Frey was the field manager, the Cubs also had a terrible Cactus League Season. But Frey stayed calm, constantly telling people, "I have a plan. I have a plan." This year Frey admitted, "I'd read a book where the guy said that to be successful, you had to have a plan, so I had to have a plan." Frey's plan, as it turned out, was to tell people that he had a plan. But other than that, he didn't have a plan. Zimmer admitted that he'd thought about that, but knew he couldn't get away with it—"The same boss is here as when he used the line."

Zimmer has been in baseball long enough to understand the importance of a manager. One day last summer, for example, he called a team meeting before a game scheduled to be played on a very windy day. "At Wrigley Field you have two kinds of games, one with the wind blowing in, the other with the wind blowing out. So I just told our hitters, don't hit any fly balls. Just hit choppers and line drives. Naturally, they listened to me."

Zimmer never let the tremendous publicity he received change him at all. After the Cubs had been swept in a three-game series by the Astros, he admitted, "They really put a whipping on us this weekend. Every move I made turned to garbage."

Zimmer's face has been described as resembling a closed fist. After seeing a particularly unflattering photograph of himself in the sports section of *USA Today*, he told his wife, "Buy one and send it to my mother. It's her fault I look like this."

The big difference between the '88 Cubs and the championship team of '89 was relief pitching. "In '88," Zimmer remembered, "if someone got into trouble as a starter, I'd look at the five men in my bullpen, close my eyes, and point. It just didn't make any difference." This season he had Mitch "Wild Thing" Williams, who promised, "Don't worry, Skip. What little hair you got you won't have when I get through with you."

But somehow Zimmer managed to stay calm the whole season. In September, when Cub fans started thinking about the magic number, the number of games that had to be won and lost for the Cubs to clinch the pennant, Zimmer admitted, "I don't even know how to figure it out. All I know is after tonight we got sixteen games left. But I don't know how to count no magic numbers. I swear I don't."

And finally, when it looked as if the Cubs were going to clinch the division title on the road, he said, "If we clinch, I don't care if it's in Tokyo."

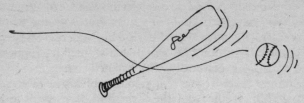

Busch Decisions

Whitey Herzog's St. Louis Cardinals chased Zimmer's Cubs all season, before fading and finishing in third place. After committing five errors during a 13–1 loss to the Mets, Herzog admitted, "We didn't pitch it very well, we didn't catch it very well, and we didn't hit it very well. Outside of that, we played pretty good."

Herzog has always been blunt with his opinions. Noting that brothers Otis Nixon and Donell Nixon were a combined 30 for 81 against the Redbirds, he suggested, "If I was managing against the Cardinals, I'd go get President Nixon from San Clemente and put him in the line-up."

When the Tigers' Sparky Anderson said he'd like to manage until he's eighty years old, reporters asked Herzog if he felt the same way. Herzog laughed. "Why would I want to do that? Sparky's only fifty-five now and already he looks eighty."

Whitey is another manager who understands his own importance. Before a big game with Houston, the Cardinals held a team meeting—then went out and lost the game. "That reminded me of the talk I gave before the seventh game of the 1985 World Series in Kansas City. It was a great talk. By the fifth inning we were down 11–0."

Loss Leaders

When the Montreal Expos were in a bad slump, manager Buck Rodgers thought he'd come up with a way to get them out of it. "Maybe I'll try voodoo," he said. Managers lose an amazing 50 percent of all the big league games played in any season. However, some managers lose more than other managers. Everybody will remember which teams won their division titles in 1989, but for the record, the last-place teams were: in the NL East, Nick Leyva's Philadelphia Phillies; in the NL West, Russ Nixon's Atlanta Braves. In the AL East, the loser was Sparky Anderson's Detroit Tigers, and in the AL West, the Chicago White Sox, managed by Jeff Torberg.

Leyva's Alone

At thirty-six years old, Nick Leyva is the youngest manager in the big leagues, although he claims that's not as young as it sounds. "I think they should count manager years like dog years—you know, multiply them by seven."

Even in spring training Leyva suspected his Phillies were in for a long season. "I told the coaches to let me pitch batting practice, because the way we were going, I figured I might be a coach again soon."

Also in spring training, the Phillies wore green uniforms in a game played on St. Patrick's Day. "We've been playing like a circus," he explained, "so we might as well wear the uniform."

Leyva noted that he had a big advantage over other managers in dealing with players who were unhappy that they weren't playing and demanded to be traded. "I told them, we're a last-place team. If you can't play here, what makes you think you can play someplace else?"

Asked why he was batting his weak-hitting shortstop, Steve Jeltz, in the number-nine spot usually reserved for the pitcher, he explained honestly, "Because there's no tenth spot."

Finally, among the things Leyva was most proud of in the '89 season was that, for the first time in his career, he appeared on a baseball card. "Nick Leyva, card no. 74. Five cents, so better get it now."

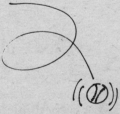

The Sparky's Gone

Sparky Anderson knew exactly how Leyva felt. The Tigers were so awful that he left the team and went home for several weeks during the season, suffering from exhaustion. After returning just in time to see his Tigers win only six games during the entire month of July, he admitted, "I doubt my mother is still reading the box scores."

After the Tigers were officially eliminated from the division race, a reporter asked Sparky how it felt to be a spoiler for teams still contending for the title. "Let me make this perfectly clear, so there's no misunderstanding whatsoever," he said. "Being 978 games out of it, as we are, I take no pleasure in the thought of destroying something nice for another team."

While Sparky was on the managerial disabled list, the team was run by coach Dick Tracewski. Explaining how it felt to manage, he said, "When I was a coach, people would walk by me without saying hello. Now they want to know what color underwear I wear."

Ah, those investigative reporters.

The Sox Are Falling

White Sox manager Jeff Torborg never overestimated his team's ability. After listening to a reporter insist that talent in the major leagues has been diluted, he pointed out, "You're just saying that because you've been watching us play for three days."

Torborg claimed his team "can lose leads faster than any team I've seen," but was particularly upset about pitchers walking the lead-off batter in an inning, who would then come around to score. "We've got that one down to a science."

Although Torborg had a long big league career, catching four no-hitters, and has coached for a decade, he's never made the kind of money players are earning today. Asked his opinion when Pete Rose was suspended, he said, "Personally, I'm not a betting man. I've never had anything to bet."

Torborg has been in baseball long enough to know that his team wasn't very good. Three weeks into the season, he conceded, "I don't think we're going to win the division. I know it's awfully early to say that, but realistically..." So he spent much of the season working with young players. Sometimes, though, he felt he wasn't getting through. During a game against Kansas City, for example, Carlos Martinez attempted to bunt with runners on first and second and nobody out. He popped the bunt into the air and it was caught in foul territory. In the ninth inning Martinez came to bat with the lead run on second and no outs, and again Torborg gave him the bunt sign. This time Martinez just watched the first pitch go by, making no attempt to bunt. Torborg immediately sent in a pinch-hitter—actually, in this case, a pinch-bunter. "I'm dumb," Torborg admitted after the game, "but it doesn't take that many times to get to me...I was so mad I wanted to kill him. But other than that, he could have stayed in the game."

Torborg is one of the brightest young managers in the game. For example, when asked by a reporter for an explanation after his team had beaten the much better Brewers for the fourth consecutive time, he said thoughtfully, "I have no idea."

Maybe Torborg should think about going into politics when his managerial career is over.

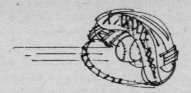

This Dodger's Blue

It was also a long season for the defending World Champion Los Angeles Dodgers' manager Tommy Lasorda, who suffered as his team finished a weak fourth. When someone, looking for a bright spot after a tough loss, said that at least the players were trying, Lasorda pointed out, "Trying's not enough. Truck drivers could try. If I brought truck drivers in, sat them down, and told them I was going to pay them $800,000 a year, they'd try from 3 A.M. until midnight. I don't want triers. I want doers. Try, hell. For $800,000 a year, I'd wrestle piranhas."

Lasorda is one of the greatest motivators in baseball history. His prize pupil this past season was pitcher Mike Morgan, who'd been in the big leagues with limited success for years, but spent the '89 season among the NL earned run leaders. He gives Lasorda a lot of the credit for that. "It started in spring training. I was in the clubhouse men's room. He came in and started screaming at me, 'You're the best. You gotta believe you're the best. If I had an arm like yours, I'd be in the Hall of Fame.'" From that point on, Lasorda became known as the Dodgers' Porcelain Preacher. And he was probably right—Morgan was the best pitcher in the men's room at that time.

Each spring Lasorda tells the young players in the Dodgers system, "If you had to go to Harvard it would cost you $8,000 a year, and when you got out, you'd have a chance to make money because you had a college education. But I want you to enroll in Lasorda U. With hard work and self-confidence and the will to make it, you'll graduate with honors and have a chance to make a lot more money than any guy who ever went to Harvard."

A prime candidate for Lasorda U. was minor league pitcher Chris Jones. Asked by Tommy where he was from, Jones replied, "Moundsville, West Virginia." I suspect bells went off in Tommy's head, lights flashed, he could see the publicity prospects standing in front of him. "What a perfect place for a pitcher to be from," Tommy said, probably sorry he hadn't created the place himself. "I'd love to live in a place called Moundsville."

But Lasorda's biggest loss this year was personal. "Tummy" Lasorda, as he was starting to be known, was so overweight that former Dodger infielder Steve Sax claimed, "I went to the beach with him and people from Greenpeace tried to roll him back in the water." And during the '88 World Series, writer Roger Angell described Tommy as "looking like a load of wet wash coming out of the dugout."

During spring training, players Orel Hershiser and Kirk Gibson bet him $30,000—to be given to a charity named by Lasorda—that he couldn't lose 30 pounds. "If I didn't have that challenge," he admitted, "I don't think I could have done it." Ultra Slimfast, a liquid diet manufacturer, offered another $40,000 if Lasorda would promote their diet. So the Great $70,000 Diet was on. Believe me, this was the only bet that was good news in baseball this year.

Lasorda weighed in at 218 pounds and the diet was on. It wasn't easy. After the first few days Lasorda said sadly, "My stomach thinks my throat has deserted it."

As weeks passed he claimed, "I see giant clams in my sleep," causing one sportswriter, Scott Newman of the

Pasadena *Star-News*, to tell him, "Now you know how those clams used to feel."

The Dodger players began wearing T-shirts pleading, "Please Don't Feed the Manager," and the diet worked. Lasorda lost 10 pounds, then 20 pounds. One day Hall of Famer Sandy Koufax walked into Tommy's office and saw him sitting behind his desk. "Where'd he go?" Koufax asked.

Never in the course of baseball history have so many people watched so few pounds disappear. The diet was all Lasorda could talk about. "Whenever I was on a diet before," he said, "I'd look down at a plate of linguini and ask myself, 'Who's stronger, you or me?' And every time a clam would look up at me and say, 'I am, fatso.'"

Eventually Lasorda lost 30 pounds, getting down to 182, and his winnings went to the Sisters of Mercy at St. Bernard's, in Nashville, Tennessee. "The only thing that ticked me off," Lasorda said after the greatest loss of his life, "is if I die, think of all the food I missed."

Lasorda was not the only manager who set out to lose in 1989. Don Zimmer, for example, went on the Nutri System diet, losing 26 pounds in seven weeks. Zimmer didn't lose as many games as Lasorda did, either. Of course, Zim had a better excuse than Lasorda. At the same time that he became Nutri System's spokesperson, he was also hired to promote Popeye's Fried Chicken, causing Jim Leyland to point out, "He's the only guy I know who gets paid to eat and diet at the same time." The "Pied Popeye," as Cubs coach Joe Altobelli nicknamed him, urged on his radio spots, "Com'on, everybody, let's chow down. Eat. Eat. Eat. Eat."

Davey Johnson of the Mets and the Padres Jack McKeon also went on diets, but the White Sox' Jeff Torborg lost weight by cutting down the size of portions, drinking iced tea instead of soda, and exercising. "I also gave up ice cream," he pointed out. "I hated that...I know where the gym is. Unfortunately, I also know where the kitchen is."

Maybe the only manager who didn't lose weight was Nick Leyva. When a Phillies coach told him that a minor league prospect had grown seven inches over the previous winter, Leyva replied, "That's nothing, I grew three inches—from a 33 to a 36."

Green Yanked

The only thing Dallas Green lost in 1989 was his job as Yankee manager. That was actually quite predictable. In the seventeen years George Steinbrenner has owned the team, the average tenure of a manager has been 154 games, or slightly less than one full season. Since 1981, the last time the Yankees won a division title, Yankee managers have lasted an average of only 125 games. Green survived as Yankee manager for only 121 days, lowering the average only slightly.

Supposedly, the day after Oakland had beaten the Yankees to end a nine-game winning streak, their longest winning streak of the season, third base coach Gene Michael left the team to attend his son's wedding. Mike Ferraro took his place. When Oakland third baseman Carney Lansford saw Ferraro coaching third, he asked him what had happened to Michael. "You know how it goes," Ferraro told him. "You guys won yesterday. Somebody had to go."

One of the first things Green did in spring training was hang motivational signs around the Yankee clubhouse. "Don't worry about the driver," one of them read. " Just load up the wagon." Another one claimed, "The person rowing the boat seldom has time to rock it." "I don't know who they motivate other than me," Green said, "but I go for that stuff."

Long before Green was fired for doing things like referring to Steinbrenner as "Manager George," it had become a long season. After the Yankees had been one-hit by Toronto's Dave Steib in early April, Green told reporters, "The way we're playing, I'm not sure we could beat Peoria." And after the Yankees had lost another game, Green promised, "This ain't the whole damn collapse of Pompeii. We'll win another game this year, let's make that eminently clear to our fans." And finally, after the Yankees had dropped their sixth game in a row and were being booed by the home fans, he said, "If I were a fan, I'd be booing, too. In fact, I'm booing from the dugout, but they can't hear me."

Green was replaced by former Yankee shortstop Bucky Dent, but things didn't change too much. "We're not hitting the ball now," Dent pointed out after another Yankee loss. "We've been defunct for the last couple of days."

A lot of people have warned Dent against signing a long-term lease, long-term meaning anything longer than 125 games. I think Steinbrenner was one of them. "On the whole," Steinbrenner said, "Bucky's done a good enough job to make him secure to start next season. After that? Well, I'm not gonna make any promises, any guarantees."

I'll make one guarantee. I'll guarantee that if the

Yankees don't get off to a good start next season, you'll by reading about the Yankees' new manager in *Baseball Lite II*.

Metso Metso

It was a much longer season in every way for Mets manager Davey Johnson, who watched his heavily favored team struggle to a second-place finish and almost lost his own job. After the season Johnson told reporters that the toughest job he ever had was working at an ironworks factory in Texas one summer. "I loaded trucks with 100-pound bags of mud, moved manhole covers, and shoveled hot coke in 110 degree heat. Believe me, I've done everything from making potholders to working at a root beer stand, and that was the toughest job." A reporter asked him what was the second toughest job he ever had. He didn't even have to think. "Listening to you guys second-guess me."

One of the major problems Johnson had to deal with was the failure of his phenom Gregg Jefferies. Jefferies had come up at the end of the '88 season and sparked the Mets to the division title. Originally Jefferies was slated to play third base, but when the Mets were unable to trade Howard Johnson and open up that spot, Jefferies was moved to second base in spring training. Johnson vowed that he would not move Jefferies from second to third. After Jefferies got off to a dismal start and was benched, Johnson tried to wake up his bat by playing him at third base. When reporters asked about that, Johnson pointed out, accurately, "I'm not moving him from second to third. I'm moving him from the bench to third."

After the Mets were eliminated for the NL East race, Johnson greeted reporters in his office with the words "Waiting for you guys to come down is like waiting in the dentist's chair for him to start drilling."

A few days later those same reporters asked him why he'd watched the televised game in which the Cubs clinched the division title. "Because," he told them, "I wanted to hurt."

LaRussa Earns an A's

The one manager who ended the season happily was Tony LaRussa, manager of the World Champion Oakland A's. LaRussa is one of only five lawyers to have managed in the major leagues. The other four, Branch Rickey, Miller Huggins, Monte Ward, and Hugh Jennings, have all been elected to the Hall of Fame. If LaRussa makes it someday, it will certainly be because of his managerial skills. He came up to the big leagues as a player with Kansas City when he was only eighteen years old. "I was overmatched in those days," he admits. "I was praying I wouldn't be used. I was always very honest with myself. I knew I couldn't play in this league."

LaRussa's A's managed to overcome injuries to several key players early in the season, as well as Jose Canseco's driving problems, to win their second consecutive AL pennant. Several people claimed that the most important decision LaRussa made during the year was forbidding Canseco to drive the team bus. LaRussa isn't a particularly strict manager, so Mark McGwire was very surprised one day when he walked into the Oakland Coliseum wearing shorts and LaRussa told him, "You can just go inside and put fifty dollars on my desk." When McGwire asked him why, LaRussa explained, "Anybody who has legs like that can't wear shorts around here."

One of the least serious injuries suffered by an A's player took place when shortstop Walt Weiss hurt himself sliding into second base. LaRussa ran out to see how badly Weiss was hurt. Later he reported "It's not serious, he just has a bad strawberry. When he slid on his leg, it burned him..." Then he smiled. "I'd like to be around when he takes a shower today." And then he stopped smiling, and added, "Don't take that wrong."

Things Are Apparently
Tough All Over

The relationship between managers and players has never been an easy one. All the manager wants the player to do is all of the things the manager couldn't do when he was a player. Except Frank Robinson, of course. Frank Robinson could do everything when he was a player. San Francisco Giants manager Roger Craig, who twice lost twenty games while pitching for the Mets, might have been speaking for all managers when he spoke to reporters about relief pitcher Mike LaCoss. "What little hair I have left is going to be gone if I keep seeing all those bases on balls," Craig complained. "In the ninth he threw strikes, which is what he has to do if he wants me to live much longer."

Pirates manager Jim Leyland had a problem with catcher Junior Ortiz, a very slow runner who desperately wanted to be allow to try to steal a base. "All right, Junior," Leyland finally agreed, "when you're at first base, look at me in the dugout. When I jump up in the air, if I don't come down, you go ahead and steal."

Managers will resort to anything to get their point across. Even Shakespeare. After the Padres had scored a team-record 17 runs against the Pirates, manager Jack McKeon told reporters, "How poor they are that have not patience." While some reporters thought he was talking about dentists, one recognized the line as coming from a play by Shakespeare and asked McKeon what play it was from. McKeon had probably been waiting, oh, fifteen years for that straight line. "Pick-off," he said.

Managing has to be the most frustrating job in baseball. As Zimmer pointed out, "I don't have a bat and I don't pitch the ball. I just get blamed when other people do."

"There are few rational things about the game of baseball," Brewers manager Tom Trebelhorn said after one game, "but tonight we played rational baseball, if that's possible." But then he put the whole game in a sort of meaningful perspective, explaining, "This game was critical to our sanity."

Angels manager Doug Rader claims managing isn't really the glamorous job that most fans believe it to be. "I've got three cars, and all of them have more than 100,000 miles on them. I've got a 'For Steal' sign on all three. I even leave the keys in the ignition. And still nobody takes them."

News was made in 1989 by managers who weren't even managing. For the first time in forty-three seasons, the last eighteen as a manager, Chuck Tanner was out of uniform. "I was so dumb that I actually thought I'd be the first manager to say, 'I retire.' Instead, I was just like every other manager. Last May the Braves replaced me. But maybe I'm not that dumb after all—they're still paying me."

Without question, the death of Billy Martin was one of the most tragic things to happen in baseball in 1989. I knew Billy well. As a manager, he never held a grudge. Before a game, he'd come up to the plate and say, "I've already forgotten how you screwed me yesterday with the worst call I've ever seen. Today's a brand new day."

Dave Righetti said, "He was the best manager I ever played for. Of course, I played for him four times." When Steinbrenner fired Dallas Green, there was speculation he'd rehire Billy for the sixth time. Many people complained. But Phil Rizzuto said, "People say he's a bad influence, but the year Billy roomed with me, I was MVP. When he roomed with Yogi, Yogi was MVP. And when he was with Mickey, Mickey was MVP. Some bad influence."

Yeah, but what I want to know is why he couldn't keep a roommate.

Every manager believes he has all the right answers. And every season one of twenty-six is proven to be absolutely correct. But when Bill "Spaceman" Lee was hired to manage the Winter Haven Super Sox in the New Florida Senior League, he announced he was going to make only one rule for his players: "If you slide, get up."

I think it's appropriate to end this discussion of managers with a classic line from one of the greatest of all managers, Casey Stengel. While Stengel was managing the Brooklyn Dodgers, outfielder Frenchy Bordagaray once reported to spring training with a full-length beard and mustache. Stengel immediately ordered him to cut them off. Speaking for all managers, he proclaimed, "If there are going to be any clowns around here, it'll be me."

Down the John

Question: Will Tommy John pitch forever?
Answer: He already has.

Certainly one of the nicest events to take place in the early part of the 1989 season was the appearance of forty-six-year old Tommy John. When John went to the mound for the Yankees on Opening Day he became the first player in modern baseball history to play in twenty-six big league seasons, tying the all-time record set before the turn of the century by Deacon McGuire.

At the beginning of spring training few people thought Tommy John would be in the major leagues on Opening Day. Even Dallas Green said he had almost no chance. In fact, just about the only person who believed in Tommy John was Tommy John. "I've just got to go out and throw well every time," he said. "And the next time, I've got to throw weller."

John's longevity was one of baseball's sweetest stories. He'd been pitching in the big leagues so long that he was the last active pitcher to have surrendered a home run to Mickey Mantle. In 1963, Tommy's rookie year, one of his teammates was the great Early Wynn. Wynn had broken into the big leagues in 1939, and one of his teammates in 1941 had been a player named Doc Cramer. As a young player, Cramer had teamed with Jack Quinn, a 1909 rookie with the New York Yankees. And playing on that Yankee team with Quinn had been the legendary hitter Wee Willie Keeler. That's five players whose careers had touched—and stretched through almost a hundred years of major league history.

One of the reasons John was able to last so long was that he always stayed in good condition. Last year he took long, rapid walks, wearing five-pound weights on his wrists. "I notice people looking strangely at me when I'm out there walking and swinging my arms and shoulders," he said. "If they keep looking, I just tell them that I'm out on a pass and lost my way back to the institution."

While most pitchers and trainers today believe in putting ice on their arm after a game to keep down the natural swelling that occurs, Tommy John has always preferred the old method of applying heat to his arm. "I prefer the whirlpool," he said, "the only place I like ice is in my Dr Pepper."

Of course, opposing managers say there's another reason Tommy was able to pitch so long—they claimed he scuffed up the ball. Tommy denied it completely. "When I pitch well, then I'm throwing spitters or I scuff it. When I get my fanny whacked, then I'm just an old man and a nice guy. I'd need a workbench on the mound to do what people say I do."

After winning the 287th game of his career on Opening Day, Tommy John was able to win only one more game for the Yankees. His record was 2–7 with an ERA of 5.80 in ten starts when he was released. Although he received no offers to pitch for another team, he's still not convinced his career is over. "I'll just pitch until someone says I can't anymore," he said, but then he added, "Or until I know I can't."

Actual-Size
Business Card of the Year

Donald Davidson is the Special Assistant to the Houston Astros' front office. He's been in big league baseball for more than forty years, breaking in as a batboy for the Boston Braves and Red Sox. He's a winner of the prestigious Bill Slocum Award for long and meritorious service to baseball, but what makes Davidson even more special is his size. Davidson is a midget. Which makes the business card he hands out even more delightful:

DON DAVIDSON
Special Assistant
to the President

HOUSTON SPORTS ASSOCIATION
P. O. Box 288, Houston, Texas 77001
The Astrodome — 713/799-9618

Weighting for
a Tall Short Story

Unlike stretch socks, baseball players come in all sizes. There is an old locker-room saying that Dallas Green missed: "It's not the size of the boy in the fight, it's the size of the fight in the boy." That's very meaningful. It's also ridiculous. You get 6'1", 228-pound Bo Jackson in a fight with 5'8" 155-pound Luis Polonia, and believe me, the size of the boys in this fight is going to make a big difference.

Size has always been a big thing for me. Obviously. This category is about the superlative players—not the best and the worst, but the oldest and youngest and biggest and smallest.

The oldest player in the big leagues last year was forty-six-year-old Tommy John, while the youngest player was the Texas Rangers' nineteen-year-old pitcher Wilson Alvarez. "Age doesn't make any difference," Alvarez said before making his big league debut against Toronto. "I know I can do the job." Alvarez faced five batters and gave up a single, two walks, and two home runs before being relieved and returned to the minor leagues. His 1989 record consisted of 26 pitches, 3 earned runs, and an ERA of infinity. The good news is he can't get any worse.

Alvarez's performance kept intact the unusual record that no pitcher born in the 1970s retired a major league batter during the 1980s. After Alvarez's appearance, Blue Jays outfielder Lloyd Moseby remarked, "It's tough. I remember my first game. But at least I made an out."

Nineteen eighty-nine was actually a grand old year. The season opened with two pitchers over forty years old, John and the Rangers' Charlie Hough, winning on Opening Day. At forty-six, John was the second oldest pitcher to win on Opening Day, behind only Phil Niekro, who also pitched for the Yankees. In Chicago, thirty-nine-year-old pitcher Jerry Reuss and forty-one-year-old catcher Carlton Fisk combined to form the oldest Opening Day battery in history. Together they were eighty-one years and twelve days old, or just two years younger than Angels coach Jimmie Reese, the oldest man still in uniform. Reuss and Fisk broke the old record, so to speak, set during World War II by the Washington Senators' Johnny Niggeling and Rick Ferrell.

Later in the season the Rangers' Hough and forty-two-year-old Nolan Ryan each started a game in a doubleheader, marking only the second time in the last fifty-six years that two pitchers over forty years old had started a doubleheader for the same team. That was first accomplished by the Yankees'—surprise—Tommy John and Phil Niekro.

For some reason pitchers seem to have longer careers

than position players. Half of the Los Angeles Dodgers' 1979 pitching staff—Hough, Reuss, Rick Sutcliffe, Bob Welch, and Don Sutton—were still pitching in the big leagues a decade later. Pittsburgh's Doug Bair was another pitcher who celebrated his fortieth birthday in 1989, causing Pirate coach Rich Donnelly to point out, "He talks a lot to our players about playing against their fathers. One day he told reliever Bill Landrum all about pitching to Billy Williams. Landrum had never heard of him. I think Doug pitched in B.C."

At the end of the '89 season Bair was a high draft choice of the St. Petersburg team in the Senior League.

The Houston Astros let Nolan Ryan sign with their cross-state rivals, the Texas Rangers, but still opened the season with the oldest pitching staff in baseball, an average of 33.4 years old. A lot of people simply called Houston's staff the Yankee staff of the future.

The oldest catcher in baseball is Kansas City's Bob Boone, who has caught more games than anyone in history. Boone, like fine wine, has gotten better with age. That's opposed to Bobby Wine, who got worse as he got older. Boone hit for about a .250 average during his twenties and thirties, but since turning forty hit almost .290. In '89 he hit .274 in 131 games for the Royals. "I've always felt I was a good hitter," he says. "I just wasn't hitting well. Unfortunately, it was that way for about fifteen years." Boone is exactly eighteen days older than Reds great Johnny Bench—and while Boone was catching 131 games this year, Bench was being inducted into the Hall of Fame.

The Reds had the most interesting blend of young and old players in '89. Before making their final cuts at the end of spring training they had eighteen players twenty-eight years old or younger and seven players thirty-five or older. The only one in the middle was infielder Ron

Oester. Speaking about playing on a team with so many older veterans, reliever Ron Dibble said, "Some of the old guys wear clothes like my father. But some of the old guys are older than my father."

One of the players beginning to become aware of the passage of time is outfielder Lloyd Moseby. After Toronto had played a long eleven-inning game against the Orioles, he pleaded, "No more extra innings. We've got too many old guys going bald."

The beginning of a new decade next season gives several players a chance to accomplish one of the most difficult feats in professional sports: playing in four different decades. Thus far ten baseball players have done it: Eddie Collins, Jim Kaat, Tim McCarver, Willie McCovey, Bobo Newsom, Jack Quinn, Mickey Vernon, Ted Williams, Early Wynn, and Minnie Minoso. Minoso really played in three decades, but has appeared in five. He made his debut in 1949 and played regularly through 1964. He appeared in three games in 1976, banging out a single in eight at bats, and went hitless in two games in 1980. He also hopes to play in a game in 1990, making him the only man to play in six decades. "But I'll only do it," he claims, "if they offer me the kind of contract I deserve."

Presenting the candidates for the four-decade club this year: Bill Buckner, Rick Dempsey, Darrell Evans, Carlton Fisk, Jerry Reuss, and Nolan Ryan. And, if somebody will give him the baseball, Tommy John.

A subject on which I happen to be an expert is weight lifting. I've now successfully lifted my weight just over the 300-pound mark. Baseball's heaviest player in '89 was probably the Milwaukee Brewers' Joey Meyer, who broke the scales at 265 pounds. During the season a group of art students attended a Brewers game and sketched several players. Nobody drew Meyer, he complained, "because they said they didn't have enough canvas." Meyer may hold a big baseball record—he may be the heaviest man to steal a base. During a game against the Mariners he was on first and there was a runner on third when manager Tom Trebelhorn signaled for a suicide squeeze play. When the pitcher went into his windup, the runner on third took off for the plate and Meyer headed for second. The pitch came in... Meyer was still heading for second. It was a wild pitch, sailing far over the catcher's head... Meyer was still heading for second. By the time the catcher had retrieved the ball the run had scored and Meyer was just reaching second. Officially, because he was running on the play, it was a stolen base—Meyer's first since 1983.

After advancing to third, Meyer scored on another suicide squeeze play. When Trebelhorn was asked after the game what would have happened if the batter had missed the bunt, he admitted, "It probably wouldn't have been a very interesting rundown."

According to Montreal Expos public relations director Richard Griffin, the San Francisco Giants set a record in '89 by starting the heaviest three-man pitching rotation ever to appear in a series against Montreal. The big three, Rick Reuschel, Don Robinson, and Mike Krukow, totaled 680 pounds, crushing by 37 pounds the record set eleven years earlier by Pittsburgh's John Candelaria, Bert Blyleven, and Don Robinson.

Nineteen eighty-nine was also a bad year for Babe Ruth. Professor Frederick Hagerman of Ohio University, an exercise physiologist, computed that the average percentage of body fat of active All-Star players is 10.3 percent. The average adult male in North America weighs in with 16 percent body fat, and estimates are that Babe Ruth carried a lot more than that. "Over the years the game has changed drastically," Hagerman said. "It's explosive now. It's mostly speed and power, and a lot of it is on artificial turf. It's highly doubtful that Babe Ruth, with the round frame of his, could be very successful in contemporary baseball." I think the doctor is absolutely right. As the old joke goes, if Babe Ruth were playing today he'd have a very difficult time—after all, he'd be ninty-five years old.

Maybe the most embarrassing thing that could happen to a position player is failing to hit his own weight. Oakland's Mark McGwire, listed at 229 pounds in the A's press guide, was hitting only .226 at one point late in the season. Determined not to be among those players who don't hit their own weight, McGwire decided, "I'm thinking about getting myself a Slim Fast commercial so I can lose a few pounds." McGwire ended the season at .231, a good meal away from hitting below his weight.

The only way I could have hit my weight was on a dart board. But here is an unofficial, partial list of those players who failed to hit their listed weights in 1989:

PLAYER	WEIGHT	AVERAGE
Joey Meyer	260	.224
Sam Horn	240	.148
Mark Parent	224	.191
Sid Bream	220	.219
Dante Bichette	215	.210
Rich Gedman	215	.212
Kirk Gibson	215	.213
Jim Traber	215	.209
Greg Walker	212	.210
Gary Carter	210	.183
Jody Davis	210	.169
*Rob Deer	210	.210
*Bo Diaz	205	.205
Matt Williams	205	.202
Jamie Quirk	200	.176
Alan Ashby	195	.164

PLAYER	WEIGHT	AVERAGE
Bruce Benedict	195	.194
Lee Mazzilli	195	.183
Shawn Abner	190	.176
Chad Kreuter	190	.152
Tom Pagnozzi	190	.150
Rick Dempsey	185	.179
Tom Prince	185	.135
Mickey Brantley	180	.157

* One pizza away

The Height of Absurdity Award this year goes to pitcher Randy Johnson, at 6'10" the tallest player in the major leagues. Johnson started the season with Montreal, but in 29⅔ innings he surrendered 29 hits, 26 walks, and 25 runs. In one game he threw a pick-off attempt into the stands on the fly, then threw a pitch so wild it hit the screen behind home plate, and, finally, forgot that there was nobody on base and pitched from the stretch position.

The Expos then traded him to Seattle as part of a package for Mark Langston. Johnson was 9–11 with the Mariners. "He's so tall," Pirates coach Rich Donnelly claimed, "that when there's a runner on second base he doesn't use a pick-off play; he reaches out and tags you."

One National Leaguer particularly sorry to see Johnson go to the American League was Glenn Wilson, who had three home runs off him. "I figure anyone 6'7" or taller, I got a good chance."

One of the shortest stories in the big leagues concerned 5'8" outfielder John Cangelosi, who was once brought in to pitch in the ninth inning of a blowout. While he was warming up he told Rich Donnelly, "I want to drop down and throw a few sidearm. I want to come in low." Donnelly paused for a moment, then reminded Cangelosi, "You're already dropped down."

The smallest spikes in the big leagues are Brett Butler's size 7. "The only one smaller I know about was Joe Morgan," Butler says. "He was a 6½. I can't even give my extra shoes away to the minor leaguer. My teammates ask if they can have the extras for their kids."

The smallest infield in organized baseball was probably put on the field by San Bernardino of the California League. The third baseman was 5'7", the second baseman and shortstop were both 5'8", and the first baseman was a towering 5'11". The shortstop, Bryan King, believes that being small was a big help on defense. "It's much easier on your back," he explained. "You don't have so far to bend down on ground balls."

"Baseball Can Be a Real Pain" Department

Even though I spent my entire professional football career on the disabled list—people thought I was blind, not stupid—the worst injury I ever had took place while I was working in Yankee Stadium. In the middle of the game I started getting very dizzy, then got a tremendous pain in my side, and finally fainted and had to be carried off the field. Well, maybe not carried, two policemen came along and each of them took a leg and they dragged me off the field. I had a badly bleeding ulcer—which I got, no doubt, worrying about the fact that I was worrying so much I was going to get an ulcer.

Football players get real he-man kind of injuries. They have an arm ripped off, they break their ears, they lose their minds—and then they're out for two games. Compared to that, some baseball injuries are really very silly. For example, the Twins' Gene Larkin suffered a pinched nerve in his shoulder while not swinging at a pitch. Chicago White Sox shortstop Ozzie Guillen split his fingernail during a game catching a throw during the most routine play in baseball—a toss around the horn after a strikeout. Reds shortstop Barry Larkin tore a ligament in his elbow during a cutoff-play competition for the fans before the All-Star Game. Milwaukee's Paul Molitor dislocated his finger while running—the player running in front of him kicked him in the hand. Maybe the most unusual medical problem is that of Reds reliever Rob Dibble, who apparently is allergic to artificial turf.

Most injuries take place during the game. Probably. Carlton Fisk, though, isn't sure exactly when he broke his hand. He believes it happened when he was jammed by an inside pitch and singled to left field. Doctors had to insert a small steel plate in his hand to repair the damage. "I don't think it'll affect his mobility," Jeff Torborg said, "but it might be a problem during electrical storms."

Years ago, after Dizzy Dean had been knocked unconscious by a thrown baseball, doctors reported, "X-rays of his head showed nothing." Some things never change. When Cubs reliever Mitch Williams was smacked behind the left ear by a line drive hit by the Pirates' Jeff King he wasn't knocked silly—he was silly even before he got hit. "I got hit in the head, the best place I could have been hit," Williams said. "Anyplace else, I might have got hurt. I saw the ball coming and I ducked into it. It was a sinker. You could call it an ugly-finder." When Don Zimmer asked Williams if he wanted to come out of the game,

Williams refused. "You've got to jump right back in the saddle," he insisted. "When I was growing up I got hit repeatedly above my shoulders by my older brother and I never shied away from him."

Well, Mitch, maybe that was your mistake.

The Yankees' Jesse Barfield suffered a slight concussion, as well as bruises to his ribs, hip, and knee, when he slammed into the outfield fence in Oakland at full speed while chasing down Terry Steinbach's triple. "There weren't too many parts of me that weren't affected," he said afterward. "I wasn't sure if I was knocked out, but Roberto Kelly asked me three times if I was all right. I only heard him once. I was saying stupid things. When they said they were going to X-ray my knee, I said, 'But I hurt my right knee.' And they said, 'This is your right knee.' And then the doctor asked me to subtract 7 from 100—I couldn't. I didn't know the answer. But I figured it out when I woke up in the morning."

That sort of makes me wonder about myself. I often say stupid things and I can't subtract 7 from 100—and the only thing I've ever run into was an old friend.

I guess playing in the outfield can be dangerous, because Andy Van Slyke ripped several layers of skin off his hand and wrist making a great sliding catch on the artificial turf at Three Rivers Stadium. "It's actually pretty interesting," Van Slyke claimed. "This injury makes me the only man in America who can take his pulse just by looking at his wrist."

Rangers pitcher Brad Arnsberg was hit directly on the shin by a Dwayne Murphy line drive. "They told me the guy couldn't hit breaking balls. I threw him a fastball and he looked at it. So I threw him a breaking ball and he crushed it." The ball, not the shin. "Most guys would've gone down from the blow," Arnsberg continued, then revealed the reason he was able to survive: "But not a double-secret ninja warrior."

As Dallas Green told several injured Yankee players in spring training, "You can't make the club in the tub." So most big league players try to play with injuries. Wade Boggs, for example, had tendon problems in both legs in 1989, causing him to complain, "I don't know which leg to limp on."

The Yankees couldn't figure out why pitcher Hipolito Peña, who had been effective out of the bullpen for them in '88, was getting hit hard in every appearance, so they ordered him to take a physical. "He hid the fact that he'd had an accident in winter ball," a Yankee official reported. "That's why we haven't seen the real Hipolito Peña. He has a broken shoulder bone, a broken wrist, and a couple of broken ribs."

Now, if Peña could hide those injuries, he shouldn't be pitching for the Yankees, he should be working for the CIA.

Few players even attempt to play with the kind of injuries suffered by Kirk Gibson. He seriously damaged his knee and shoulder during the '88 playoffs against the Mets, and those injuries didn't heal over the winter. Most people believed he'd start the '89 season on the disabled list, but instead he was in Tommy Lasorda's Opening Day lineup. "I believe what you talk about happens," he said. "If you say you're not going to be ready, chances are you're not going to be ready. Four days before Opening Day I realistically didn't think I was going to be ready, but I told myself I would be." Asked if his knee or shoulder was causing the biggest problem, he replied, "It doesn't matter. I'm a mess."

I like that philosophy. I'd like to believe that whatever you talk about happens. Because just yesterday I was talking about Raquel Welch delivering a brand-new car to my house as a gift. If it works for Gibson, maybe it'll work for me, because I have a lot in common with Kirk. I'm a mess, too.

Obviously, there are a lot of injuries that can't be overcome, no matter how much a player wants to be on the field. As Dodgers pitcher John Tudor, who missed the entire '89 season with an arm injury, explained, "It only hurts when I throw a baseball, which, unfortunately, is what I have to do to live."

A lot of young players just waiting for their big break got them during the 1989 season—arms, fingers, toes. Among the stars who spent a good part of the '89 season on the disabled list were Jose Canseco, Andre Dawson, Gibson, George Brett, Dave Winfield (who missed the whole season), Eric Davis, Andy Van Slyke, "Oil Can" Boyd, Carlton Fisk, John Candelaria, Mel Hall, Jim Gott, Keith Hernandez, Gary Carter, even Dwight Gooden, who said, "If this is what it feels like to be retired, I don't think I'm ever going to."

I suspect the team that suffered the most injuries the last few seasons has been the St. Louis Cardinals. One year they lost starting pitcher Danny Cox when he fell off a three-foot-high retaining wall. Another season they lost their ace, John Tudor, when the opposing team's catcher slid into the Cardinal dugout trying to catch a foul ball and shattered Tudor's knee. They even lost star outfielder Vince Coleman for the playoffs one year when he was swallowed up by the automatic tarpaulin monster. During 1989 they lost starting pitchers Greg Mathews and Danny Cox for the whole season and almost everybody else on the pitching staff spent time on the disabled list, in addition to several position players who spent time on the DL. "What does it all mean?" Whitey

Herzog asked. "It means that if World War III breaks out we win the pennant by twenty games. Because not one of our guys could pass the army physical."

In 1989 the Cardinals were not the only team to lose key players to injuries. Pittsburgh, for example, put six starters on the disabled list in the first two weeks of the season. The situation got so bad for the Pirates that relief pitcher Brian Fisher threw a wild pitch while warming up in the bullpen—and it bounced all the way into the dugout and smashed pitching coach Ray Miller in the nose.

The Milwaukee Brewers had nine players on the DL at one point during the season, including five injuries that put players out for the remainder of the season. Things got so bad for the Brewers that when second baseman Billy Bates, called up to replace Jim Gantner, who was lost for the year with a knee injury, suffered a first-degree separation of his shoulder, he kept playing. "A first-degree separation is mild," trainer John Adam explained, "if it happens to somebody else."

A lot of players were injured off the field. Yankee rookie pitcher Dave Eiland missed several appearances in spring training after cutting a finger on his pitching hand trying to open a crab claw at dinner. The Cubs' Rick Sutcliffe missed a start when he was bitten by his own dog—a perfect example of injury added to insult. "The dog got into a fight," Sutcliffe explained, "and I tried to break it up and I got bit." Toronto reliever David Wells lacerated the thumb on his pitching hand when he smashed a window while walking in his sleep. A few weeks later he fell down during another sleep-walking excursion. But even after both incidents Wells claimed he wasn't worried about the dangers of these nocturnal strolls, saying, "I'm not going to lose any sleep over it." But he also said he was going to sleep on the first floor.

Another Blue Jays pitcher, Mike Flanagan, was injured when he slipped on the floor of his hotel bathroom and hit his eye on the shower door. "It took me a little while, but I finally figured out how it happened," he explained later. "David Wells was sleep-walking and he pushed me through the door."

I always knew pitchers didn't like to take showers; now I know why. They're obviously pretty dangerous. The Mariners' superb rookie outfielder Ken Griffey, Jr., fractured his right hand stepping out of his hotel bathroom shower. "It's pretty disappointing," Griffey said, "but there's nothing I can do. All I can do is look forward to returning to the team. And hopefully, they can play better without me."

I love that quote. When was the last time a player hoped a team would be improved by his absence?

This year, at least, the most dangerous game for baseball players turned out to be golf. Well, not golf exactly, but golf equipment. The Angels' Wally Joyner reinjured a badly sprained ankle in a pro shop when he tripped over the corner of a floor mat. Nobody ever accused the Red Sox Mike Greenwell of being fast, but he missed a game when he was hit by the golf cart that was picking up the protective screens used in batting practice. I guess, in golf, that's what's known as a reckless driver. Brian Fisher suffered the golf injury of the year when he was injured playing miniature golf. How can you possibly get hurt playing miniature golf? I figured the worst thing that could happen to someone on a miniature golf course is that they'd suffer a small injury, but Fisher sustained a thirteen-inch gash on his left arm when the golf club he was leaning on snapped and sliced his arm.

Maybe the only nice injury story of 1989 was the comeback of Mets pitcher Bobby Ojeda, who had cut off the tip of the middle finger of his pitching hand while clipping hedges at his home just before the '88 playoffs. The tip was surgically reattached, but a lot of people doubted Ojeda would ever be able to pitch effectively again. After he proved he could still pitch during spring training, the Mets rewarded him with a $3 million, two-year extension to his contract. Then he went out and compiled a good 13–11 record and a 3.47 ERA. "I have so much praise for Dr. Eaton," Ojeda said of the surgeon who saved his career, "I should do commercials for him. The reason I feel no difference now is that he's such a genius. Of course, I'm not going to buy him a new car."

Commercials? That is a commercial I think I'd like to hear: "If you happen to cut off the tip of your finger with a hedge clipper, try Dr. Eaton. I do every time."

It wasn't only players who got hurt in '89. My friend Kenny Kaiser, the wonderful American Legue umpire, was very lucky he wasn't seriously injured when he was hit in the throat by a foul tip. "The doctor said if it had been another inch higher, it could've crushed my windpipe. That's nice to hear, isn't it?"

Actually, that's just the translation of what I think Kenny said. What he really said was "Arrrghhhhh. Ooooohhhhh. Ggggghhhhlllll."

The Yankees' sixty-three-year-old special advisor Clyde King fractured five ribs when he felt out of a tree house. When coach/broadcaster Lou Piniella heard about that, he said he wasn't surprised because "George Steinbrenner has Clyde looking for talent everywhere." So don't be shocked if the Yankees announce they've signed Tarzan. Or better, the way the Yankees have been playing lately, Cheetah.

Of course, he who laughs last laughs hardest. A few weeks later Piniella sprained his left foot playing racquetball and was on crutches for a few weeks. Kaiser didn't laugh, though. He just went, "Gggggha ha, grrrrrha ha."

Certainly one of the closest calls was the very mild heart attack suffered by Brewers broadcaster Bob Uecker. After returning to the radio booth, and to his Miller Lite commercials, and to his popular TV show, *Mr. Belvedere*, and to the numerous personal appearances he makes, Uecker said, "It's great to be able to go to the ball park again. I tell you, if I'm going to blow out someday, I want it to be at the ball park. Really, it'd be great. I'd blow out, they'd cart me around the field a couple of times, the fans would cheer, and then, poof, out the main gate. Gone.

"After I had the heart attack I woke up in the hospital and saw the flowers, but I couldn't hear any music. I thought my wife had bought me a cheap funeral.

"The doctors have got me on this high-fiber diet, but I'm a little nervous about the side effects. I've noticed that dogs are beginning to sniff my legs." Uecker also claimed that he'd started exercising, and had taken up running. "Before this, my feeling had always been 'Hey, I've got a car. Why do I need to run?' But I've changed my approach."

San Diego reliever Dave Leiper had a heart attack scare. After suffering from an irregular heartbeat, he was told by a doctor, he "might have to change careers. The doctor said I may go out on the field someday and drop dead." That was some doctor. That kind of advice would have given me a heart attack just from worry. It was later determined that the irregular heartbeat had been caused by a virus, and Leiper was permitted to pitch. Other than that, Leiper had a pretty boring winter.

One of the things I did during the winter was work as a spokesperson for the great Fisher Nut Company. When you talk about nuts, you're talking about those people at Fisher. One of the things I've learned while working for Fisher is that nuts are an important health food. Young nut eaters concerned about heart attacks should start by eating one handful of nuts and eventually work their way up to three or four a day, because nobody wants to go too nuts in the beginning.

I could make nutty jokes all page.

There are a lot of different ways players deal with injuries or medical problems. For example, Pirates coach Bruce Kimm was with the team on an airplane soon after having had arthroscopic knee and elbow surgery. The Pirates assistant trainer suggested Kimm elevate his leg. "Gee," Kimm asked, "how high do you want it? It's already at 33,000 feet."

The Mets' Howard Johnson had problems with a tightness in his arm early in the season. It started as a stiffness in his shoulder, then moved down to his biceps, his forearm, and finally his fingers. The Mets trainers couldn't find anything wrong with him. "Whatever it is," manager Davey Johnson said, "it needs to be exorcised. We need a Catholic priest."

Although baseball teams provide their players with the most modern medical equipment available, some players still prefer home remedies. Yankee Roberto Kelly, for example, treated a sore wrist by wrapping garlic around it. Asked by reporters what the garlic was for, Kelly said, "I'm not telling." It's pretty obvious to me what it was for: to keep the reporters away.

The Giants' Most Valuable Player Kevin Mitchell's wrist was so sore that "even my glove hurt when I put it on." He treated it by rubbing on an ointment made for him by his grandmother. "That's what grandmothers are for," he explained. The remedy was made from the contents of her kitchen cabinet, Mitchell said, including tequila. Now, that's one kitchen cabinet I'd like to see.

Mitchell has always had his own method for treating medical problems. Like millions of other people, he often uses Vicks Vaporub to clear up congestion. However, not like millions of people who rub it on—as the directions advise—Mitchell dips his fingers into the jar, then sticks his fingers down his throat. "It clears you up pretty quickly," he claims. "I just think that, instead of using Vicks candy, why not go right straight to the point?"

The day after the Yankees put outfielder Mel Hall on the fifteen-day disabled list with a badly strained hamstring, he was walking around the clubhouse without a limp and seemed to be almost fully recovered. Hall claimed that he had been cured by a mysterious "woman from the Far East," who'd delivered his room service breakfast to him. After telling him she'd been watching the game on television and seen him hurt himself, she claimed she could heal him. "She started messing with the nerves and the joints in my foot for about twenty minutes," Hall explained, "then told me I could get up and walk. And I did."

When teammate Rickey Henderson heard that story, he really didn't believe it. "Right," he said, "and I'm on cloud twenty-three."

There are probably a lot of people who would tell you that Henderson is absolutely right, but I'm not sure. That's certainly not the first time I've heard about a woman telling a man to take a walk.

Return of a Giant

My candidate for the Comeback of the Year Award is the Giants' Dave Dravecky. In 1988 surgeons removed a large piece of cancerous muscle from Dravecky's left biceps, and told him he'd never pitch again. But Dravecky was determined to prove them wrong. When his rehabilitation sessions began in January, he couldn't even lift up his pitching arm without help. Gradually, he strengthened his muscles, but most people believed Giants manager Roger Craig was right when he said, "The first pitch he throws is going to be a miracle."

Yet after three starts in the minor leagues, he returned to the Giants. When Kevin Mitchell saw the long scar on Dravecky's arm he said, "My God, it looks like Jaws took a bite out of you." On August 10 Dravecky started against the Cincinnati Reds. "You have to appreciate what he's done," sympathetic Reds manager Pete Rose said before the game. "You have to pat him on the back...and hope he gets beat today."

Dravecky retired the Reds on nine pitches in the first inning, then threw a one-hitter for seven innings, leaving the game after giving up a three-run homer in the eighth, but earning the victory. "It's a great story," one Giants fan said, but then put the whole thing in proper perspective: "But the most essential thing is that the Giants get a healthy pitcher for the stretch drive."

In his next start, against the Expos, Dravecky had a three-hit shutout going into the sixth inning. Then he gave up a home run to Andres Galarraga and hit Tim Raines with a pitch. Finally he threw a wild pitch, then tumbled forward onto the infield grass. His comeback, and his career, were over. His left arm had been fractured. His teammates surrounded him and carried him off the field on a stretcher.

Dave Dravecky finished his final season with a record of 2-0 and a 3.46 ERA, but this is one case where the numbers don't begin to tell the story. I didn't have to be a bad math teacher to know that.

When the Giants clinched the pennant several weeks later Dravecky ran onto the field to celebrate—and during the celebration he was accidentally hit from behind and refractured his arm. At the end of the season he announced his retirement from baseball.

Collect Calls

When I owned my sporting goods store, people would often come in and ask me if I had any autographed baseballs in stock. "Sure," I'd tell them, "they're all in the back. Who would you like?"

Then they would say something like, "You wouldn't happen to have any Sibby Sistis, would you?"

I'd snap my fingers, "Boy, are you in luck. I've got one left." Then I'd go into the back, where my mother was sitting in front of a little black-and-white TV set sewing a shawl, and say, "Ma, I need a Sibby Sisti." She'd put down her shawl, pick up a baseball, and sign "Sibby Sisti." I mean—I'm being very honest—does anybody know what a real Sibby Sisti signature looks like? When I gave the customer the ball everybody was happy.

But in those days collecting baseball memorabilia was a hobby; today it's a billion-dollar business. Had I known that was going to happen, I would have had my mother signing Sibby Sistis all day. Today bats, balls, cards, old uniforms, anything signed or worn by a big leaguer, or used in a major league game seems to have great value. During the Pete Rose investigation in 1989, for example, it was revealed that Pete knew the value of the uniforms he was wearing in the games in which he banged out each of his record-breaking hits—so between innings he'd go into the locker room and change jerseys, giving him six or seven different jerseys to sell for each hit.

Baseball cards have joined the ranks of stamps and coins as legitimate collectible items. At least five different companies are currently issuing full sets of baseball cards, while other manufacturers put out specialty cards to take advantage of the market. In the world of collectibles, mistakes become instantly valuable, usually because the mistake is corrected as soon as it is discovered, limiting the number of the original item. Sure, as soon as I get out of baseball, mistakes become valuable. Believe me, if mistakes had been worth money while I was working, I could have been a wealthy man.

But because mistakes are worth money to collectors, probably the most valuable card issued in 1989 was the Fleer Company's Billy Ripken card. On the card Ripken is shown holding his bat on his shoulder, a very common pose. But written in Magic Marker on the bottom of the bat knob is a two-word obscenity, a phrase that once would cause mothers to wash their children's mouths out with soap for saying it, but that now earns young comedians an hour on cable television. "I had no idea that was written on the bat when the picture was taken," Ripken said. As soon as Fleer realized the problem existed, it recalled the cards that had already been circulated and tried to correct the mistake, tried to correct the mistake, tried to correct the mistake...It actually tried to correct the mistake six different times, so that there are now seven different Billy Ripken cards, each of them in limited supply and therefore valuable. Ripken got more publicity from his obscene baseball card than from his playing ability.

Fleer's first attempt to correct the card consisted of simply scratching out the two words separately, but the letter *F* remained faintly visible. Next the words were scratched out with a single, looping stroke. Then the words were covered with a small black box. Then the black box was enlarged. Next an unsuccessful attempt was made to air-brush out the offending words—the result was that the words became visible again. Finally Fleer just punched a hole in the card.

Billy Ripken's card was worth more than fifty dollars. In fact, it became so valuable that the learned Judge Wapner was called upon to settle a dispute over ownership of a Billy Ripken card on *The People's Court*. Judge Wapner was amazed to find out that the card was worth so much money. "You mean to tell me that one Billy Ripken is worth fifty dollars?" he asked. "Why, his brother is much better than he is."

The Ripken @#%$#$ was not the only mistake card manufacturers made in 1989, just the most publicized. Fleer also mistakenly used Randy Kutcher's picture on its Kevin Romine card and had to change Neil Allen's residence from Sarasota, Florida, to Syosset, New York.

Score cards had their own touchy problem. In the background of Tiger pitcher Paul Gibson's card, another player can be seen with his hand on his private parts, making them public. When Score discovered the mistake, it air-brushed out the offending hand, making the original card more valuable. "Someone suggested we might have done it on purpose," a spokesperson for Score said, "but that's ridiculous. We certainly didn't say, 'Now, you stand there and hold your crotch while we take the picture.'"

Upper Deck's Dale Murphy card was reversed to show him as a left-hander. Upper Deck also mistakenly printed Shawn Hillegas on the front of its Brian Holton card and Ronn Reynolds on the back of Bill Schroeder's card. Upper Deck can't even positively identify the Cub shown on the back of Gary Varsho's card—the only person they know it isn't is Gary Varsho.

But probably the most unusual card printed this year is that of minor leaguer Keith Comstock in a special Las Vegas Stars set issued by ProCards. On the card Comstock is shown standing straight up, his arms spread wide apart, just about to be hit in the crotch by a baseball.

Would I make something like that up? Well, yeah, I would, but not in this case. This is absolutely true. This is the first baseball card that is actually painful to look at. But unlike the player in the background of the Gibson card, this was no mistake. "Players can pose any way they want to," ProCards representative explained, "and this was the way Comstock wanted to be remembered...When we checked with the team, they insisted that we had to use it."

Until recently, it hadn't bothered me that I'd never appeared on a baseball card. For some reason the card companies preferred to issue cards showing players. But their definition of a player is being stretched. The Ball Four

Company put out an eleven-card set in 1989 titled "Legends of Minor League Baseball." And among those legends was Cuban Premier Fidel Castro. The truth is that Castro never even played minor league baseball. Maybe he saw a few minor league games when the Havana Sugar Kings were in the International League, but that shouldn't count. "He was actually a lousy pitcher," a spokesperson for the card company admitted. "He insisted all these years that he could have made it in the major leagues, but he was terrible. Scouts said he was an erratic sidearmer with little control. When he pitched for the military team in the sixties he was routinely shelled, but the manager wasn't about to send the dictator to the showers."

Castro shelled? Bad choice of words, Mr. or Ms. Spokesperson. Other players in this set included Pete Gray, the one-armed outfielder; Joe Hauser, who hit 399 minor league home runs, and Smead Jolley, who had a great name.

But still no Luciano. Okay, maybe I don't mind Castro, and maybe I don't mind Smead Jolley, but a Baltimore company even issued a "Famous Rabbi" series in time for Passover, and I didn't make that set either. When I asked about it, they said I didn't have a prayer.

I admit, that last part isn't true. But the rest of it is.

The card business has grown so rapidly that in order to compete successfully some new cards have to do something besides being cards. For example, one company issued battery-operated cards that, when inserted into a device that could be bought at a toy store, actually told you about the player pictured on the card. There are cards that come with little statues of the players—fortunately, there is no Keith Comstock statue. And finally, there is the world's heaviest baseball card. No, I told you, there is no Luciano card. This is a seventy-five-pound steel replica of the Topps 1965 Jake Wood card created by sculptor Robert Spinazzola. Can you imagine some kid trying to flip that one?

The five most valuable Bob Uecker cards are Topps 1962, which is valued at $125; 1966, $60; 1964, $50; 1965, $40; and 1963, $30. But the most valuable baseball card of all is the rare 1910 Honus Wagner "tobacco card," which Wagner had withdrawn from circulation because he didn't want to encourage kids to chew tobacco. "Old T206" is supposedly worth as much as $130,000 in mint condition. There are fewer than fifty of these cards known to exist, but what looked like the Steal of the Year took place in West Pittsburg, California. A fourteen-year-old boy who had been given a 1910 Wagner by his grandfather (now deceased) to be used to pay for his college education, took it out of the family Bible and brought it to school to be photographed. The photographer hit him over the head with his camera and escaped with the card.

The good news, or maybe it was the bad news, or maybe it was good news for the boy and bad news for the thief, or maybe it was bad news for everybody, is that it was later discovered that the card was actually a replica of the original and was worth no more than $10. "I'm glad it's a phony," the boy said. "At least we didn't get ripped off for 130,000 big ones."

Maybe the only big leaguer who really understands how I feel about not being pictured on a baseball card is Davey Concepcion. The great Reds shortstop, after a career of almost two decades, was omitted from the 1989 Topps set. When he reported for spring training, a representative of the company told him, "We apologize for leaving you out—we thought you retired."

Autographs also remained a very big business in 1989, and Hall of Famers were paid as much as $10,000 to appear at collectibles shows. The value of a player's signature, like the value of cards, is in direct relationship to his success on the field. There are some players, though, who are still willing to sign their name for free. Believe me, my signature isn't worth anything; it isn't even worth anything when it's on a check. Maybe the business of selling signatures isn't a bad thing, but it has certainly changed the age-old tradition of youngsters collecting the autographs of their heroes and hanging them on their wall. When a young fan approached Hall of Famer Warren Spahn and asked for his autograph, for example, Spahnie was a little surprised and probably a little pleased. He pointed out to the young fan that he hadn't even been born when Spahn was starring for the Braves. "Oh, that's okay," the kid explained politely. "You're getting old and you're going to die soon and your autograph is going to be valuable."

Sometimes a player doesn't even have to be old to be old. When Johnny Bench visited the Hall of Fame a few weeks before he was to be inducted, he was approached by a thirteen-year-old girl who asked, "If you really used to play pro baseball, what's your name?"

"I'm Johnny Bench," he said proudly.

"Do they call you that because all you can do is sit on the bench?" she asked, giggling.

Bench thought about that for a few seconds, then replied, "Is that how you act when they make you repeat first grade?"

Look, there's a reason he was a catcher and not a squat-down comedian.

Probably the most valuable pieces of baseball memorabilia sold this year were the original 3″ × 5″ unsigned paintings used by Topps on their 1953 card series. Some of these portraits were auctioned off by the company, with a portion of the proceeds being donated to charity. The Mickey Mantle painting was sold for $121,000, and the original Willie Mays went for $88,000, both of them to the Marriott Corporation, which intends to display them in a traveling exhibition. Jackie Robinson sold for $78,000, Whitey Ford went for $35,200, Bob Feller for an even $33,000, and Roy Campanella was sold for $15,500. The only thing I know about art is that I don't know anything about art, but I wonder if this is as much as has ever been paid for 3″ × 5″ portraits by mostly unknown and unidentified artists.

In that same auction, a 1952 contract between Mantle and Topps sold for $17,600, and a contract between Mays and the Bowman Card Company went for $14,300—far more than the contracts had been for.

The Play's Some of the Thing

There were approximately 109,512 outs recorded in the major leagues in 1989, give or take a double-play. And some of them were a little more complicated than others. I'd like you to do something for me: close your eyes and count to three. You can use your fingers if you need to. I'll wait. (Dum, de dum, de dum, dum dum.) Now, that wasn't too difficult, right? Well, maybe not for you, but it wasn't quite so easy for some big league ballplayers to remember that the other team gets three outs every inning. That's three. Innings never go on sale. Three outs, always. John Kruk, as I explained, caught a fly ball in the outfield and held on to it as Bobby Bonilla scored from second base. After the game Phillies coach Larry Bowa tried to simplify things for Kruk. "From now on," he said, "before each inning we'll give you three sticks of gum. After each out, stick a piece of gum in your mouth. When you're out of gum, it's time to come in."

Personally, I'm not sure that was such a good idea. Have you ever tried to put twenty-seven pieces of gum in your mouth at the same time?

Of course, Kruk wasn't the only player who suffered from this problem. Hey, these guys are paid to play, not count. The White Sox' Steve Lyons, for example, was playing first base when he forgot how many outs there were. After the second out was recorded at first base, Lyons casually flipped the ball to first base umpire Terry Cooney—who leaped out of the way of the ball as if it were a dinner check. By the time Lyons realized what had happened and recovered the ball, the baserunner had gone from second to third.

The Braves' Gerald Perry was on first base with one out when a teammate hit a routine fly ball to left field. Perry put his head down and started running. He rounded second and headed for third. He rounded third and charged home—and when he got there, he was informed that he had been doubled off first base. Now, that's when he should have kept running.

But the greatest play that never happened in 1989 took place during a Mets-Giants game in June. With two outs in the bottom of the ninth and the score tied 1–1, the Giants' Ernest Riles was on first base and there was a count of one ball and two strikes on batter Kirt Manwaring. Mets reliever Randy Myers stretched, checked Riles at first, then started to throw to the plate. Riles took off for second base. Myers threw, Manwaring swung and missed. Catcher Barry Lyons's throw to second sailed into center field. Riles rounded second and headed for third. Center fielder Lenny Dykstra charged the ball and scooped it up. Riles rounded third and kept going. Dykstra pumped once, twice, then threw a perfect strike toward the plate. Lyons caught the ball on a bounce, Riles slid, Lyons sprawled in the dirt and tagged him. Home plate umpire Jerry Layne checked to make sure Lyons had held on to the ball, then shot his right hand high into the air and called Riles out...the fourth out of the inning.

Manwaring had struck out to end the inning before the play had started. "I knew the play was over when the batter swung," Lyons claimed. "I threw mostly for practice."

"I knew the play was over," Dykstra also claimed, "but when you see a ball loose like that you're supposed to get it."

In the Mets dugout, coach Bill Robinson claimed, "We're management. We knew there were three outs. We're supposed to know things like that."

In fact, apparently the only people who didn't know there were three outs were the people not even involved in the play, Mets broadcasters Fran Healy and Rusty Staub. About fifteen minutes after the play had ended, in the middle of the tenth inning, after repeated showings of the replay, Staub admitted, "We've just received word about the play that ended the ninth inning..."

Wrong, Rusty! The strikeout ended the ninth inning. The rest was just an encore. Actually, it could have been worse. Riles could have beaten Dykstra's throw to the plate. What would have happened then would have been something to see.

As I said, these guys are paid to play, not to count. The umpires are paid to count. By hey, we all make mistakes.

In the sixth inning of a Cubs-Pirates game, Mark Grace was at bat with a count of one ball and one strike. As the pitch came in, the runner took off from first base. Grace swung and missed, ball two, and the runner was safe at second. That's right, swung and missed, ball two. That's what the home plate umpire called it, so that's what it is. I admit that it probably wasn't the correct call in this particular circumstance, in any circumstance actually, but all these people were yelling at the home plate umpire. You'll notice I haven't identified the home plate umpire. There is a very good reason for this. I don't want to.

Two pitches later, Grace walked on what should have been ball three. One pitch later, Pirates manager Jim Leyland protested, but his protest was not allowed. "They told me my appeal was too late since another pitch had been made," Leyland said. "I don't know if that included the strike that was a ball. I told them they should get it right and not penalize me."

"I could see Leyland's point," the batter, Mark Grace, admitted. "He saw me swing. But the only guys that count are the guys in blue."

That's correct, but sometimes they don't count so well. No real damage was done, however, as the Cubs didn't score that inning. But after the game, Don Zimmer claimed, "That call changed the whole complexion of the ball game." Um, okay, Don, how?

So maybe some players aren't so good counting outs and some umpires aren't so good with strikes, but innings? Everybody knows that a baseball game consists of nine innings. Well, almost everybody knows. Oakland rookie Jim Corsi had just been brought up from Tacoma in time for a game against the Yankees. Corsi was so excited when Rick Honeycutt got the last out of the eighth inning that he was the first one out of the dugout to congratulate him on the victory. Also the only one.

Honeycutt looked at him, then asked, "They only play eight innings in Tacoma?"

When Honeycutt got the final out an inning later, several Oakland players told Corsi, "Now, Jim, now!"

Once, years ago, Mets reliever Larry Bearnarth was pitching with the bases loaded and manager Casey Stengel took the long, slow walk out to the mound to give him some advice. When he got there, Casey looked at Bearnarth and said, "Hubba, hubba," then turned around and went back to the dugout. Bearnarth's next pitch was lined into a triple play to end the inning. When Bearnarth got back to the dugout, he went over to Casey and asked, "What does 'Hubba hubba' mean?"

Casey shook his head. "Goddamn triple play."

The triple play is still one of the rarest plays in baseball, but there were several turned during the 1989 season. Probably the most unusual one took place during an Astro-Padres game. Kevin Bass was on third and another Houston runner was on second. The batter smashed a line drive to third base for one out. The third baseman whirled and threw to second to double up the runner for the second out. And meanwhile, Kevin Bass was tearing for home. Unfortunately, he'd neglected to tag up at third base. The second baseman threw to catcher Mark Parent, who tagged Bass to complete the triple play. "I forgot how many outs there were," Bass admitted later, but then explained that he had a good excuse. He said he'd been to the doctor's office earlier in the afternoon and taken a complete physical, "and maybe they took too much blood out of me."

Parent was asked if he'd ever seen a triple play. "No," he said, "I've never seen one, but I'm sure I've hit into a few."

Which makes me wonder where he was when he hit into them.

Even more rare than a triple play is the fourth legal out of an inning. This is a play that every umpire learns about in umpire school, but never sees take place on the field. In my entire career, I never saw it happen once. Well, it didn't happen in 1989 either, but it could have. Instead, the reverse happened: a run scored after the inning had ended. In fact, it scored so long after the inning had ended the fans in the ball park didn't even know it had scored until they read the newspaper the next day. With one out in the eighth inning, the Yankees were leading the Brewers 4–1, with Mike Pagliarulo on third and Bob Geren on first. Manager Dallas Green gave batter Wayne Tolleson the suicide squeeze sign.

Tolleson popped up his bunt attempt. Pitcher Jay Aldrich caught the ball in the air. Pagliarulo, running on the pitch, had no chance to get back to third, so he just kept running toward home plate. Aldrich ignored him and instead threw to first base to double up Geren, who was also going, for the third out of the inning. But unknown to everybody in the ball park, except home plate umpire Larry Barnett, Pagliarulo had touched home plate before the double play had been completed. So even though Pagliarulo had left his base too soon, because it was not a continuous-action double play his run would count unless the Brewers made an appeal at third base before every infielder, including the pitcher, had crossed the foul lines into foul territory. How many of you knew that? Be honest. Now, how many of you really knew that? "That's covered in rule 7.10d," Barnett explained after the game. "It's the apparent-fourth-out rule where the defense has to appeal the play. Milwaukee had to throw the ball to third base for what would be a legal fourth out. Then they can choose to make that the final out of the inning to prevent the run from scoring. But Milwaukee didn't do that, and it's not my job to tell them. The Brewers left the field without making an appeal, so the run counted."

You'll notice that in this case I've identified the umpire. Thank you.

But because Barnett didn't make a real strong point of notifying the official scorekeeper, the run wasn't posted until after the game, making the final score 5–1. So every one of the almost 25,000 fans in the ballpark went home without realizing they'd seen one of the most unusual plays in baseball take place. "I'll tell you what," Dallas Green said afterward, "I've been in this game for thirty-three years, and I've never, ever, ever seen that play."

"I haven't seen that play in my twenty-six years in baseball," Larry Barnett said. Of course, I've got them both beat: I still haven't seen that play.

That was a case of not seeing something that wasn't there. Obviously. But the Reds' Todd Benzinger didn't see something that was there—the Reds' Barry Larkin. Benzinger was on second base with two out and Cincinnati trailing Montreal 6–3 in the sixth inning. Benzinger noticed that Expos pitcher Pascual Perez really wasn't paying too much attention to him, so he slowly edged off second, he stretched his lead another step, and another half-step, and when Perez kicked his leg into the air to throw his pitch, Benzinger put his head down and dashed for third. He dived into the base—safe! Benzinger had surprised everybody in the ball park, but most of all he had surprised his teammate, Barry Larkin, who was quite happily occupying third base at the time. It has not been recorded exactly what Larkin said to Benzinger. Perhaps it was something like, "Fancy meeting you here," or, "Come here often?" or "%@$!@%@!, you lunkhead." Larkin took off for home plate but was tagged out in a rundown.

After the game Benzinger tried to explain his strategy. "I just know that when I was on second, I got a great jump on Perez. I had to go. Perez forgot all about me— but then again, I forgot all about Larkin." Benzinger added that he had assumed Larkin had scored on the previous play, a ground ball to the infield. "I did it for the sake of the team." Okay, it's a little different, but maybe it worked. The Reds scored 16 runs in the next three innings to win the ballgame.

Just when you think you haven't seen everything, something else happens that you've never seen before. And you still don't see it. For example, the Phillies were trailing Montreal 3–2 in the ninth, with Bob Dernier on first and Von Hayes at bat. Hayes hit a long fly ball to right field, Hubie Brooks backed up against the wall and leaped high into the air, his glove extended as high as he could reach, and...and...and the baseball disappeared. Brooks didn't catch it, it didn't rebound off the fence, it didn't go into the stands. Nobody could find it. "I kept running," Dernier said, "but I knew something weird was happening."

First base umpire Tom Hallion raced out to right field and demanded of Brooks, "Okay, where's the ball?"

"I'll tell you one thing," Brooks told him, "there's no way that's a home run. I don't know where it is, but it's got to be here somewhere."

Hanging on that right field fence was the Expos' 1981 division title pennant. After a prolonged search, Brooks ripped the pennant off the wall, and the ball rolled free. The umpires ruled it a ground-rule double and sent Dernier back to third. It didn't make any difference in the ball game. Randy Ready followed with a single to score Dernier and Hays to win the game. Under different circumstances, this could have been the first time that a team lost the pennant because they'd won the pennant.

The problem is that baseballs have a tendency to go precisely the places where nobody expects them to go. In Darryl Strawberry's glove, for example. One night in the Kingdome the Mariners' Dave Valle hit a tremendous drive that should have gone into the seats for a home run—instead, it hit one of the speakers hanging 132 feet above the infield and dropped almost straight down. The ball bounced off the outfield wall and White Sox outfielder Ron Kittle played the carom perfectly. His throw to the plate was in plenty of time to nail Valle, who was trying for an inside-the-park home run. Of course, in a domed stadium like the Kingdome, every home run is an inside-the-park home run. I just wonder if someone was smart enough to name that speaker that robbed Valle of a home run Tris. Or if from now on it's going to be known as Death Valle.

Look, there was a reason I became an umpire and not a comedian. Of course, there are some people who will claim I became both.

There is one play in baseball that is almost impossible to mess up. This is so easy it's not even called a play. I have another test for you: hold out your right arm. Congratulations, you have now signaled for a right-handed relief pitcher. Would you like to try it again? Here's the variation: hold out your left arm. This is not really very difficult. Even you can do it. In ideal circumstances the manager or pitching coach walks out to the mound and signals to the bullpen, using his right arm or left arm. So far there are no computers that have mastered this particular program. The only rule a manager has to remember is that a team is permitted only one visit to the mound each inning, and that a pitcher must face at least one batter before he can be removed. Got it? Right arm, left arm, one trip, one batter.

Every year some manager signals for a pitcher he

doesn't want or makes two trips to the mound in the same inning. I remember when Jim Fregosi was managing the White Sox. I was working third base. Salome Barojas was pitching. A coach went out to the mound to talk to him, but when he got to the mound he realized he couldn't speak Spanish, so he motioned with his right arm for the Spanish third baseman to come to the mound to interpret. And a few seconds later, from the bullpen located right behind third base, the right-handed reliever came jogging in.

The 1989 version of this play was just a little more complicated. The Twins were beating the Red Sox in Minnesota one night, and they had two runners on base with one out. Twins manager Tom Kelly sent left-handed-hitting Jim Dwyer to the plate to pinch-hit. Boston manager Joe Morgan countered by bringing in left-handed-throwing Joe Price to pitch to Dwyer. Dwyer tried to bunt Price's first pitch, but thought he'd managed to check his swing. Home plate umpire Greg Kosc called the pitch a strike. They argued briefly, then Kosc threw Dwyer out of the ball game. This is when the situation started to get really interesting. Tom Kelly sent right-handed-hitting Carmen Castillo to the plate to replace Dwyer. Morgan went to the mound and brought in right-handed Mike Smithson to pitch to Castillo. After Smithson had thrown six warmup pitches, Kelly reminded the umpires that a pitcher had to face a minimum of one batter, and Price had faced only one batter.

No, that's not right. What I mean is, a pitcher has to face one complete spot in the batting order, no matter how many different players occupy that spot. Theoretically, a manager could send up a different hitter on every pitch. Although the basic rule of umpiring in complicated situations is penalize the team that has made the mistake, and in this case the Twins were gaining an advantage because their player had been thrown out of the game, crew chief Larry Barnett agreed with Kelly. "I haven't seen that play in my twenty-six years in baseball," he said. "I just waved in Smithson instinctively."

Barnett sent Smithson back to the bullpen and recalled Price from the dugout to finish pitching to that spot in the order. "There have been games when I know the manager would have liked to send me back where I came from," Smithson said after the game, "but this is the first time it's actually happened."

Everybody argued. Price solved the problem by striking out Castillo, proving the importance of platooning. Later in the game, Morgan successfully managed to bring in Smithson. In the umpires' dressing room after the Twins had won the game, umpire John Hirschbeck held on to his rule book while he discussed the play with reporters. "We know in our minds what we based it on," he said, then frowned, and added, "but I suppose you guys want rules..."

Price pointed out that he had done his job, but admitted, "It's kind of hard to keep from laughing."

Here is your final test of this section: If A is scheduled to bat before B, when does A come to bat? Take your time, think it over. I'll repeat the question: If A is scheduled to bat before B, when does A come to bat? Time's up. The correct answer is—before B. Maybe you thought it was a trick question.

There really aren't too many things a player has to actually remember during a game: don't scratch certain places when the camera is focusing on you, make sure you go to the back of the dugout if you're going to smoke a cigarette, go to bat when it's your turn. It just isn't that tough. But every season several players somehow manage to bat out of turn, and it becomes the umpires' job to figure out what to do about it.

In 1989, for example, Houston's Rafael Ramirez actually made an out without even batting. That happened because, before the game started, Astro manager Art Howe changed his usual batting order, switching Ramirez and Alex Treviño. Apparently these players weren't aware of it. I don't know what they were doing, maybe they were scratching the places you aren't supposed to scratch when the camera is focusing on you, but Treviño came to bat in Ramirez's scheduled spot. Then he proceeded to complicate matters by getting a base hit. When the opposing team protested that Treviño had batted out of turn, the umpires, carefully schooled in this precise situation, got it absolutely wrong. They decided it was a double play, ruling that Treviño, who had singled, and Kevin Bass, the next scheduled batter, who hadn't done anything yet, were both out. I have no idea how Bass got caught. Finally, after Howe appealed, the umpires got it right. Ramirez, who was sitting comfortably by himself in the dugout, bothering no one, was ruled out for not batting, and Bass, the scheduled hitter, was put in the batter's box. Treviño's single was erased and he was not credited with an at bat.

I'd like to see Abbot and Costello try to figure out who was supposed to be on first on that play.

The Blue Jays also batted out of turn one day, but by the time the Brewers caught them, the regularly scheduled next batter had taken a pitch, making it too late for them to protest. The fact that Brewers manager Tom Trebelhorn failed to catch Toronto was surprising, because he happens to be sort of an expert on this particular rule. Once, when he was managing in the minor leagues, he had a very short player named Mack Harrison on his squad. Harrison had made the final out in the eighth inning, but when the opposing team brought in a wild relief pitcher to start the ninth, Trebelhorn sent Harrison up to bat again, ordering him not to swing at a pitch until the count reached either three balls or two strikes. Now, maybe the manager of the other team knew that Harrison was batting out of turn—but if he did, he was smart enough not to protest until Harrison had completed his at bat. According to the rules, if he had protested while Harrison was still at bat there would have been no penalty; the regularly scheduled batter simply would have gone to bat and assumed the count on Harrison. But if he waited until Harrison completed his turn at bat and then protested, he was guaranted an out no matter what Harrison did. Treblehorn didn't allow that to happen— when Harrison had three balls on him, Treblehorn called time and sent the regularly scheduled hitter to the plate to complete the at bat. That batter walked on one pitch, and there was nothing the other manager could do about it. To me, that's the baseball version of going through the yellow light. It's not exactly legal, but if you don't get caught, if helps you get where you want to go.

Comic Reliever

Relief pitchers have become the professional wrestlers of major league baseball. So many of the great relievers have become known as much for their characters as for their pitching ability. It wasn't just Al Hrabosky, for example, it was "The Mad Hungarian." Every time Sparky "The Count" Lyle came in to pitch, the organist played his theme song, "Pomp and Circumstance." Rollie Fingers used to stand on top of the mound twirling his handlebar mustache. The animated Tug McGraw had a nationally syndicated comic strip, "Scroogie." The Yankees star reliever of the 1950s, Ryne Duren, had an interesting act: he threw about a hundred miles per hour and pretended to be almost blind. So it is now my great pleasure to give the 1989 Comic Reliever of the Year Award to...Mitch Williams of the Chicago Cubs!

One of the most popular movies of the year was a baseball spoof entitled *Major League*. A principle character in that picture was a relief pitcher nicknamed "Wild Thing" because of his lack of control. When he came into a game, the fans would sing the old Troggs song "Wild Thing." Naturally, when the picture became a hit, relief pitchers in several cities tried to become the "Wild Thing." But only Mitch Williams really earned it.

Williams, who claimed that "I pitch like my hair's on fire," was second in the NL with 36 saves, but as Earl Weaver once said about him, "He's more dangerous than smoking." Williams was a wild thing in '89, surrendering 52 walks in only 81.2 innings. When Williams was out of control, he was terrible. For example, he came into a game in '89 and hit the first two batters he faced, threw a wild pitch, walked the next batter, committed a balk, then walked a fourth batter. After the game he admitted, "I'm just glad nobody got hurt."

Obviously, he isn't the only one. Facing the Pirates' Andy Van Slyke, Williams almost hit him with his first two pitches, fell behind in the count 3–0, then came back to strike him out. "If everyone was like him," Van

Slyke said, "I think I'd find a safer way to make a living."

Against the Reds in Wrigley Field one day, he surrendered two hits and three walks and hit two batters—but gave up only one run. When he came into the Cubs' dugout at the end of the inning, all of his teammates were wearing their batting helmets.

Williams is quite candid about his lack of control. Picked for the NL pitching staff in the '89 All-Star Game by manager Tommy Lasorda, Williams said, "Before the game Tommy asked if any of us had a trick pitch, and I said, 'Yeah, I'll throw a strike once in a while.'" When asked by a reporter which one of his pitches was the most difficult for him to throw, he thought for a few seconds, then said, "A strike."

Cub fans loved him, naturally. Chicago's marketing director, John McDonough, claims that Williams is personally responsible for an increase in ticket sales. "He's more thrilling than Boris Karloff and more exciting than Michael Jackson," McDonough said.

Williams came to the Cubs from the Texas Rangers in a nine-player deal after the '88 season. While in the American League he proved to be, statistically, the toughest pitcher in baseball in night games. Throughout his entire career, opposing batters hit only .189 against him under the lights. So it is somewhat fitting that he was traded to the Cubs, the only team in baseball to play the majority of its home games in the daytime.

Williams hadn't really liked playing in Texas, explaining, "Some of my relatives thought that a Texas Ranger was a cop." Apparently he wasn't one of the most popular members of the Rangers. After Texas reliever Jeff Russell had described Williams as a selfish player, the "Wild Thing" said, "He's not the first guy who's called me a jerk... But we're still friends."

I wonder what his enemies think about him.

Twice in 1989 Williams saved games without retiring a single batter. Early in the season he came into a game against San Diego with two on and two out in the ninth inning—and before he threw his first pitch, he whirled around and picked Padre Carmelo Martinez off second to end the game. "Letting a guy swing the bat," he explained, "...always is dangerous."

Then, in the middle of the Cubs' stretch drive, Zimmer brought him in to face the Expos, who had two on and two out, with the Cubs leading 4–3. This time he threw one pitch. Then he went into his stretch, and instead of firing a pick-off throw to first baseman Lloyd McClendon, he just lobbed the ball toward first. Base runner Jeff Huson was so surprised he didn't react. McClendon raced in behind him, caught the ball on one bounce, and tagged him out to end the ball game. "We were very lucky," Williams admitted.

Although Williams's most important hit of the season was a three-run homer in a critical game against the Mets, he also received a lot of publicity when he hit a rat with his bat, then told reporters, "I've always been a low-ball hitter." Williams also boasts that he is the only major leaguer with a tattoo of the cartoon character Speedy Gonzalez on his calf. "My dad has one," he told reporters, "and so do my brothers. Our family has never been accused of being all there."

Particularly, I sort of suspect, when they're together at the very same time.

Making the Big Score

There were approximately 2,106 major league games played in 1989, and every one of them was unique. But some games were more unique than others. For example, the biggest inning of this season, or just about any season, took place on August 3, when the Cincinnati Reds scored 14 runs on a modern major league record 16 hits—in the first inning of a game against the Astros. They held on to win, 18–2. "I've never seen anything like that," Houston manager Art Howe said after the game. "Sixty-three pitches before we got the first out."

"Every time I went to sit down," the Reds' Rolando Roomes remembered, "I had to get back up and shake somebody else's hand." In the inning the Reds' 14 runs scored on 16 hits—and no walks. "Why would they want to walk?" asked Expos pitcher Bob Forsch, who gave up 10 hits and 7 runs in the inning.

The Reds set five records; among them: their 16 hits in an inning broke the record of 14 set by the Red Sox in 1953; their 12 singles broke the record of 11 in an inning shared by the 1925 Cardinals and 1953 Red Sox; 7 Reds had 2 hits in the inning, which broke the mark of 6 set by the Cubs 106 years ago. Luis Quiñones tied a major league record by batting three times in an inning—but his presumably once-in-a-lifetime opportunity to get three hits in an inning ended when he flied out his third time at bat to end the inning. The 14 runs were one short of the all-time record for runs scored in an inning, a mark set by the Dodgers in 1952—against the Reds.

Pitcher Jim Clancy led off the game by walking Mariano Duncan, who then stole second. Luis Quiñones bunted for a base hit, Duncan moving to third. Eric Davis singled, Duncan scored, and Quiñones moved to second. 1–0 Reds. Ken Griffey homered, scoring Quiñones and Davis in front of him. 4–0. Rolano Roomes beat out an infield grounder. Todd Benzinger singled; Roomes went to third. Jeff Reed singled, scoring Roomes, Benzinger stopping at second. 5–0.

Bob Forsch was brought in to relieve Clancy. Clancy's ERA boomed from 4.43 to 4.95.

Ron Oester doubled, Benzinger scored, and Reed stopped at third. 6–0. Forsch threw a wild pitch, Reed scored, Oester went to third. 7–0. Pitcher Tom Browning grounded to first base for the first out of the inning.

Duncan doubled to right, Oester scored. 8–0. Quiñones singled; Duncan stopped at third. Davis singled, scoring Duncan; Quiñones stopped at second. 9–0. Griffey singled, Quiñones scored, Davis went to second. 10–0. Roomes got his second infield hit of the inning, moving Davis to third and Griffey to second.

Astro manager Art Howe went out to the mound and told Forsch he had to stay in the game because the Reds were short of pitching. "I'm well aware of that," Forsch told him; "I'm not trying to do this."

Benzinger doubled, clearing the bases. 13–0. Reed singled; Benzinger stopped at third. Oester singled, scoring Benzinger; Reed stopped at second. 14–0. Browning singled, moving Reed to third and Oester to second. That meant that, in their second time through the batting order, all nine Reds had hit safely—a probability that was computed to be 1 in 909,091. Duncan flied out. Two outs. Quiñones flied out. Three outs, finally. I got tired just writing it all down.

"Everybody was a superstar today," Roomes said. "We couldn't wait to get to get up to hit. I've never seen anything like it."

And, except for the several thousand people in attendance at the Dodgers-Reds game in 1952, nobody else has either.

The inning took 38 minutes to play, and Cincinnati raised their team batting average for the entire season three points. At the end of the inning, Benzinger said, "I looked up at the clock and thought, 'This is going to be a pretty long day.' " Of course, not as long as it would have been if Benzinger had been playing for the Astros. Ironically, the rest of the game was completed in a very fast hour and 38 minutes. The total time of the game, 2 hours and 16 minutes, made it the shortest game played in the big leagues that day. If the first inning was projected over a whole game, the Reds would have scored 112 runs on 128 hits. And that is assuming that the Astros didn't score 110 runs in the ninth to tie the game and force the Reds to bat in the bottom half of the inning.

Forsch pitched 7 innings, giving up 10 runs on 18 hits, and saw his ERA rise from 4.12 to 4.80. That's the most hits ever given up by a Houston pitcher, topping the old record of 16 that had been set by Don Wilson in 1970.

Do you think, just maybe, at the end of the game, as the Astros were trudging back into the locker room, somebody shouted, "We'll get them tomorrow"?

The Astros also played the longest game of the year, in time and innings, when they beat the Dodgers 5–4 in 22 innings. Two months after that game the Dodgers raised their '89 record in 22-inning games to 1–1 when they beat Montreal in 22 innings, 1–0.

The Astros-Dodgers game lasted 7 hours and 14 minutes, making it the longest night game in NL history, the longest game ever played by both of the teams, and only nine minutes shorter than the longest major league game in history. The Dodgers used 23 of their 24 players on their roster; the Astros used 21. Houston managed to get the winning run to third base 5 times after the seventh inning and twice had runners thrown out at the plate trying to score on a sacrifice fly; the Dodgers got the potential winning run to third 3 times. Dodger catcher Mike Scioscia was supposed to have taken the night off—instead he caught 17 innings, went 0 for 5 at bat, and was involved in three big collisions at home plate.

The losing pitcher was Dodger third baseman Jeff Hamilton, who relieved Cy Young Award winner Orel Hershiser in the 21st. Hamilton became only the third non-pitcher in the last 21 years to get a decision, joining Rocky Colavito and Jose Oquendo. Although Hamilton's fastball was clocked by the radar gun at 91 mph, he complained, "I really didn't have my good pop out there tonight." This was Hamilton's first appearance on the mound since his senior year in high school. "I was working on seven years' rest," he pointed out. Houston's Ken Caminiti was so upset when Hamilton struck him out that he snapped his bat over his knee.

The winning run scored when Rafael Ramirez lined a single off the glove of first baseman Fernando Valenzuela, scoring Bill Doran from second base on a very close play at home plate. "I was really too tired to argue the call," Scioscia admitted. "Fred [umpire Fred Brocklander] said he touched the plate. There was so much confusion at the time I didn't have the angle to see it." Or maybe the energy.

"This is worse than a World Series loss," Hershiser contended. "It becomes almost more than a game. It has sentimental value because we played for so long." Sure, he says that now, but will he show up for the reunion?

Of all the players in that game, Dodger outfielder John Shelby probably had the longest day—going an even 0 for 10 at bat.

The very next day the Dodgers and Astros played a piker's 13 innings. Houston won again, 7–6, their 10th straight victory, on pitcher Mike Scott's sacrifice fly.

The Dodgers beat the Expos 1–0 in their 22-inning game, the second longest shutout in baseball history. Montreal pitchers set a record by throwing 22 innings, facing 77 batters, without giving up a single walk. The game apparently ended in the 16th inning when the Expos' Larry Walker scored from third base on a short sacrifice fly, making a great slide to evade the tag attempt of Dodger catcher Rick Dempsey. The Expos poured onto the field to congratulate Walker, and three of the four umpires left the field and headed for their dressing room. But the Dodgers appealed that Walker had left third too soon, and—in what must have been one of the most agonizing decisions in the history of exhausted umpires—Bob Davidson made one of the great calls, upholding the Dodgers' protest and calling out Walker for leaving the base before the ball had been caught. As Willie Randolph said, "I don't remember ever winning a game that we'd already lost."

The Dodgers almost won the game in the 18th when Eddie Murray hit what should have been a run-scoring double, but the first base umpire ruled that outfielder Larry Walker—again—had caught his long fly ball. TV replays showed that the ball actually bounced off the outfield fence into Walker's glove. The umpire taketh away, the umpire giveth.

The oldest player in the game, thirty-nine-year-old Rick Dempsey, put the Dodgers ahead in the top of the

22nd with a home run off his former Oriole teammate Dennis Martinez, who was making his first relief appearance in six seasons.

The time of the game was a smooth 6 hours and 14 minutes, or exactly one minute longer than it took Montreal to fly to California after the game. "And," according to Expos PR director Richard Griffin, "no one scored a run on that flight, either."

I also want to give credit to the broadcasters. Because Dodger announcers Don Drysdale and Vin Scully weren't at the game, Ross Porter had to do the entire game by himself. Mr. Ed was a talking horse—Ross Porter got hoarse talking. Rene Cardenas, who teams with Jamie Jarrin on the Dodgers' Spanish broadcasting network, went down to the field in the bottom of the eighth inning to prepare to do the post-game interviews, and waited there 14 innings while Jarrin did the game alone.

Nineteen eighty-nine was also a year in which no lead, no matter how big, was really safe. In June, for example, the Red Sox jumped out to a tidy 10–0 lead against Toronto, but the Blue Jays came back to win 13–11 in 12 innings. That 10-run lead was the largest ever lost by the Red Sox, although they have blown 9-run leads three different times. That game also marked the 12th straight time the Blue Jays had beaten the Red Sox in Fenway Park. If that wasn't a record, pizza isn't health food.

The very same day that that game was being played, the Yankees took a 10–0 lead over the Brewers. But as the scoreboard told the story of the Boston-Toronto game, Milwaukee kept chipping away at the Yankee lead. New York's relief pitching proved to be too tough for the Brewers, though, as the Yankees held on to win, 12–9.

Three days later, just three little days later, the Pirates scored 10 runs in the first inning of their game against the last-place Phillies in Philadelphia. That was the Pirates' biggest inning in forty-seven years, and it seemed as if that it might be enough runs for them to break a six-game losing streak. In fact, the 10-run lead seemed so secure that Pirates broadcaster Jim Rooker told his partner in the booth, John Sanders, "If we lose this game, I'll walk home." To Pittsburgh.

And then the Phillies started their comeback. Von Hayes and Steve Jeltz each hit two home runs. The switch-hitting Jeltz hit one from each side of the plate, the first Phillie in history to accomplish that rare feat. The thing that made it even more unusual is that Jeltz hadn't hit a home run in five years, covering 1,357 at bats.

"I felt secure about my statement until the sixth or seventh inning," Rooker said. "Then I broke into a cold sweat."

Eventually, the Phillies tied the score at 11–11, then went ahead on Darren Daulton's two-run single in the eighth, and finally won the game 15–11. In a strong contender for the Understatement of the Year, Pirate starting pitcher Bob Walk said, "When you score ten runs, you should win."

"It was very painful" was all Pirate manager Jim Leyland could say after the game. But not nearly as painful as it would be for Jim Rooker. After the season, on October 5, Rooker started to walk home from Philadelphia. Along the way he collected pledges for several Pittsburgh charities.

"Rook's Unintentional Walk" took twelve days and covered exactly 337 miles. When he finished, Rooker said, "I feel great—from the ankles up. From the ankles down, I feel like I've been stabbed by an ice pick."

But Rooker had learned his lesson. Several weeks after the Phillie game, the Pirates again took a 10–0 lead, this time against the St. Louis Cardinals. Rooker's broadcasting partner, Lenny Frattare, teased him, suggesting, "If we lose this game..."

Rooker cut him off. "If we lose this game," he said, "our road record will be 11–23. There's only room in my mouth for one foot." This time the Pirates held on for a 12–4 victory.

For a team that finished last in its division, the Phillies could score a lot of runs. Of course, with a pitching staff that had the highest team earned run average in the National League, they had to. In what might have been the highest-scoring game of the year, for example, losing 10–3 to the Cubs, they battled back to win 16–13 in a 35-hit ball game played at Wrigley Field. Actually, the fact that these two teams slugged it out shouldn't be much of a surprise. As everybody knows, the Phillies and Cubs have played the two highest-scoring games in major league history: in 1922 the Cubs edged the Phillies, 26–23, and the Phillies nipped the Cubs 23–22 in 1979. Both of those games were also played at Wrigley Field. Now, I don't know for sure, but I would sort of guess that there was a breeze blowing out during those games. In fact, my guess is that there was a hurricane blowing out during those games.

The Reds, who had scored those 14 runs in one inning, found out how it felt to be in the other dugout one day against the Giants. Cincinnati led 8–0 after six innings, and Giants manager Roger Craig threw in the rosin bag, taking out his regulars and putting in his second-line players. But the irregulars came back to score 9 runs and win the ball game, 9–8. The Giants used twenty-five players in the game, including four different people in the lead off spot in the order, three catchers, three shortstops, and six pitchers. A seventh pitcher, Scott Garrelts, was used as a pinch-runner. Craig called it the greatest win of his managerial career, and catcher Terry

Kennedy celebrated by taking the entire team out to dinner.

Some seasons are pitchers' years, and runs are tough to score. Some seasons, but not 1989. Nineteen eighty-nine was a hitter's year. For example, after Kansas City had dropped a squeaker to Cleveland, 17–5, while Bo Jackson—who also played pro football during '89—was out with an injury George Brett admitted, "I knew we were in trouble because the only player we have who can score touchdowns was on the bench, and we didn't have time to kick four field goals."

A careful observer probably could have figured out that it was going to be a long season for the Tigers when they were edged, 14–0, by the Twins in the fourth game of the year. "The Tigers had plenty of opportunities in this game," Twins manager Tom Kelly contended. "A couple of hits here and there and it's a real good ball game."

Sure it is. Nice try, Tom. But I preferred to believe the statement made after that game by Tigers manager Sparky Anderson, who said, "As far as I'm concerned, they're the best team of all time."

For the record, the Red Sox led the major leagues in scoring in 1989 with 774 runs, while the Braves were last with 584. But probably the most unusual scoring record of the season belongs to the Milwaukee Brewers, who scored seven runs in seven straight games, and won them all. The most unusual line score of the season showed the Seattle Mariners scoring 2 runs on one hit and no errors to beat the Texas Rangers, who had no runs on 13 hits and an error. This was the second time in four seasons that Rangers knuckleballer Charlie Hough had lost a one-hitter.

The Mariners scored their first run in the sixth inning when Harold Reynolds singled for their only hit, went to second on a balk, went to third on a wild pitch, and scored on a sacrifice fly. They added another run in the seventh on a walk, a stolen base, and the only error of the game. With no runs on 13 hits, the Rangers came within a hit of tying the all-time record for the most hits without scoring a run, a feat that has been accomplished by the 1913 Giants and the 1928 Indians. After the game, Rangers manager Bobby Valentine said in frustration, "I guarantee you'll never see another game like this one."

And Seattle's happy manager Jim Lefebvre said happily, "That's what makes this game so damn interesting."

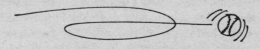

They're Called Owners Because They Do Things Their Own Way

From 1909 until George Steinbrenner purchased the team from CBS in 1973, the New York Yankees made only seventeen managerial changes. In 1989, with the firing of Dallas Green and the hiring of Bucky Dent, the Boss proved he could do in only sixteen years what it had taken other people sixty-four years to accomplish. Some people would say that's progress; most people would say that's George Steinbrenner.

It was another tough year for baseball's most controversial owner. After being severely criticized for firing Green, Steinbrenner appeared on the ABC news show *Primetime Live* to defend himself. When host Sam Donaldson asked him how it felt to be booed by Yankee fans at Yankee Stadium, the Boss explained, "Loving in sports is winning...I could play Hitler in right field if we were winning, and the fans would cheer."

Steinbrenner added that Stadium security people had assured him that only about 1,000 of the 43,000 fans in the ball park were actively participating in the "George Must Go!" chants that rocked the Stadium. "That's okay," Steinbrenner continued, "that's their right. I'm not mad. The only way you get me mad in a situation like this is to ignore me. They pay their money; they would probably boo the Pope."

Well, that would probably depend on how well he was hitting.

I know how tough New York fans can be; remember, I was the umpire who called out Lou Piniella at home plate in a playoff game because his leg had gone *over* the plate instead of touching it to cost the Yankees the game—but cheer Hitler and boo the Pope? I don't know. Boo Ed Whitson maybe, but not the Pope. Even Yankee fans aren't that tough—unless you call out Piniella for going over the plate.

The 1989 season got off to a rough start for Steinbrenner. At a charity auction at the Yankees' spring training headquarters in Fort Lauderdale, a picture of George was offered for bids. Someone immediately shouted, "Twenty-five cents," causing the auctioneer to ad-lib, "It's amazing how Dave Winfield can throw his voice." The picture was eventually purchased by a man named Bob Quinn, who claimed the one thing he had always dreamed about owning, since he was a tiny little child, was a nice picture of George Steinbrenner. And purely coincidentally, Quinn just happened to be the Yankees general manager at the time. He paid twenty dollars for the picture.

Early in the season the Yankees' popular public relations director, Harvey Greene, announced that he was resigning to accept a similar job with the pro football Miami Dolphins. Greene once said that Steinbrenner was such a demanding boss that he wasn't allowed to get sick during the baseball season. Asked to recall the silliest thing that had happened during his three years on the job, Greene said, "My second week with the Yankees I had a nine o'clock curfew during spring training. I found out about the curfew the day I turned thirty-three. I called home and told them I was allowed to stay out later than that when I was thirteen years old and had my bar mitzvah."

Later in the year Steinbrenner was mad at the New York sportswriters—presumably because they ignored him—and decreed that he would only answer questions submitted in writing, and would do so at his convenience. He also stated that he would not answer questions about certain subjects, among them the feud he was having with Dave Winfield concerning the disposition of funds Steinbrenner had agreed to contribute to the Dave Winfield Foundation. Naturally the reporters covering the Yankees agreed to abide by these rules, and submitted a list of twenty questions to the Boss: (1) What do you remember about your first time at the circus? (2) Why was Lou's hair so oily? (3) How much does the moon weigh? (4) Is Ricky Henderson (a) an MVP candidate, (b) an illiterate, or (c) neither? (5) Do you like Jell-O? (6) When was the last time you saw Margo Adams? (7) What's the flip side of "Wipeout"? (8) Is the Pope Catholic? (9) Why is peanut butter so sticky? (10) Did you ever punch a doggie? (11) Can you core a apple? (12) What do you think of Deion Sanders's jewelry? (13) Who framed Roger Rabbit? (14) What makes Dallas Green? (15) What's a hen way? (16) What's the capital of Montana? (17) When'd ya get down? (18) If you could be a tree, what kind of tree would you be? (19) Do you floss? (20) Have you ever bowled?

There is no record of the Boss responding to these questions.

From the beginning of spring training some people were wondering how long the stubborn Dallas Green would survive as Yankee manager. By August the Yanks were fading out of the race, Green was referring to Steinbrenner as "Manager George," George was referring questions from reporters about Green to the Yankee publicity department, and the reporters were referring to Green as "the soon-to-be former Yankee manager."

Green was fired in August, along with most of his coaching staff. Six-foot-seven, 255 pound Frank Howard was one of the most popular members of that staff. After promoting Dent, Steinbrenner offered Howard Dent's former job as manager of the Yankees' Triple A affiliate in Columbus. Howard turned it down, mostly out of loyalty to Green, and suggested, "Let him [Steinbrenner] talk to me."

The Boss somehow took that as a threat. "Guys don't scare me," he said. "I would have seen him... Frank Howard can stick it in his ear."

But, believe me, only if he really wants to. Mr. Steinbrenner, here's a word of unsolicited advice: taking on the Pope is one thing, but Frank Howard?

Toward the end of the season Steinbrenner criticized some of his fellow owners for the large contracts they were offering their players. That was quite surprising, especially considering that other owners have long accused Steinbrenner of forcing up salaries by overpaying free agents. "I've got to laugh at some of the salaries [they're paying]. We're one of the few teams that has shown any restraint this year. I doubt if we have more than one player in the top ten this year...We've got to operate like a business. They [the other owners] don't have to worry about the [$500 million] TV contract blowing anybody out of the water."

Sure. Steinbrenner ended 1989 by signing free-agent pitcher Pascual Perez, who was 9–13 with Montreal, to a three-year contract worth almost $6 million.

The Boss was not the only boss to have a tough year. In Cincinnati, owner Marge Schott suffered through the Pete Rose investigation, then watched her team fade out of the pennant race. At one point during the season she met with her team and suggested that a few prayers might help them start winning, causing third baseman Chris Sabo to point out, "I don't think God really cares whether we hit or not. If God cared, Billy Graham would hit .400."

Schott has occasionally been compared, both favorably and unfavorably, to her always present pet St. Bernard, Schottzie. One night in Cincinnati the Reds were supposed to play the Cardinals, but the start of the game was delayed more than two hours because of a rainstorm. Only two innings after the game began, it started raining again. After another hour-and-a-half delay, the game was finally called off. For some reason, the Cardinals' pitcher Joe Magrane blamed the whole thing on Marge Schott. "I've heard the phenomenon before of a master taking on the physical appearance of the dog," he said; "that's already established. But I've never heard it went as far as the master taking on the thinking process of the dog."

Schottzie refused to comment on that accusation.

New owners in baseball in 1989 included Indianapolis businessmen Michael Browning and Jeff Smulyan, who purchased the Seattle Mariners. Among the first things they did after their purchase had been approved by the

American League was assure Mariners fans that the team was going to stay in Seattle. Or at least try to do that. Proving he was going to fit right into the American League, Browning said reassuringly, "This team is not going to be the Seattle Mariners. It's staying right here in Indianapolis."

A group that included the oldest son of President George Bush, George W. Bush, and Bill DeWitt, Jr., whose father once owned the Cincinnati Reds, bought the Texas Rangers and Arlington Stadium for $80 million. "I talked to the President about throwing out the first ball," George W. reported, "and he kept talking about wanting to play first base. I said, 'We've got a first baseman.' He hung up."

I think I can understand the President's response. If his family is the First Family, if Barbara Bush is the First Lady, if their dog, Millie, is the First Dog, then why can't he be the first baseman? Apparently he has some hang-up about it.

The Orioles were bought for $70 million by a group that included R. Sargent Shriver, the 1972 Democratic candidate for Vice President, and Larry Lucchino. Lucchino is no relation to me.

Yet.

Before the 1989 All-Star Game was played at the California Angels' Anaheim Stadium, Angels owner Gene Autry was honored at Disneyland with a big party that featured the Disneyland dancers, singers, and hostesses, all dressed in Old West saloon waitress costumes. "The Cowboy," as Autry, baseball's oldest owner, is known, looked down at the girls and said "I never saw so many pretty girls. It's like looking at a garden of flowers." Then, proving his eyes are still in big league condition, he added, "Well, maybe there are a few weeds out there."

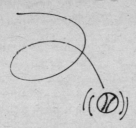

Off with His Head

For as long as most people can remember, baseball and beer have been a popular combination; of course, the more beer people drink, the less they can remember. This year Houston's slugging first baseman Glenn Davis objected to that relationship, specifically to the fact that every time he hit a home run, Astros broadcasters would offer the toast of their sponsor: "Glenn Davis, this Bud's for you." So, like Honus Wagner, who objected to his picture on a card being used to sell tobacco in 1910, Davis announced he wanted no more toasts. "I know [beer sponsors] put a lot of money into baseball," he said, "but as a player, I feel I have the right not to be associated with it. I spend a lot of time talking with kids, telling them not to drink. I don't want to be a hypocrite in their eyes."

Several beer brewers suggested that if Davis really felt that way, then he should do something meaningful— stop hitting home runs! Well, maybe they didn't. The club did not agree with his sentiments, but respected his wish. Of course, some newspaper reporters wondered what Davis would do if he was traded to the Milwaukee Brewers, asking, if he gave in to them, would that be considered a concession stand?

But then an incredible thing happened: other players around the league agreed with Davis and owners stopped selling beer in their ball parks, voluntarily giving up the millions of dollars in revenue they received from beer sales.

And Pete Rose really believes it's a sure thing he's going to be reinstated.

The truth is that most people didn't agree with Davis. The Brewers' Cris Bosio, for example, replied when asked what he'd be doing if he weren't a ballplayer, "I would be driving a beer truck in my hometown of Sacramento. I've always wanted to do it, and I think it would be a fun job."

In Seattle, before owner George Argyros sold the team, he had a disagreement with the operators of the Kingdome, who put a seventeen-game ban on selling beer in the stands, forcing consumers to go to the concession stands for their brews. "They just don't vend," he said. "I looked around Saturday night and didn't see anyone except a peanut man."

Well, maybe if his teams had been a little better, more people would have come to the ballpark.

In Chicago, the Tribune Company, owners of the Chicago Cubs, prohibited beer consumption in the visitors' clubhouse. When the Pirates came to town, they responded by refusing to speak to *Tribune* reporters. When a reporter from another paper asked the Pirates' Andy Van Slyke how his bat felt during a game played in near-freezing weather at Wrigley Field, he replied pointedly, "Like a cold beer."

And finally, the Reds were in San Francisco in July when an earthquake—much milder than the one that rattled the city during the World Series, but still pretty scary—shook their hotel and woke them up in the middle of the night. "At first I thought I'd had too many Coronas," reliever John Franco said, mentioning a local beer, "but then I realized it couldn't be that, I only drink light beer."

If They Spend So Much Time There, Why Isn't It Called a Clubhome?

There is one thing I've wondered about since I started in baseball. In the clubhouse, or locker room, the lockers are actually large cubicles, they don't even have doors—in fact, the one thing lockers can't be is locked.

You're probably wondering why I've wondered about that. It's because baseball players spend a tremendous amount of time in the clubhouse. And much like high school students, their lockers become very personal; they decorate them with pictures, sentimental items—in the case of the Phillies' Roger McDowell, snakes...

Of course, some lockers are much luckier than others. In the Red Sox clubhouse, for example, Wade Boggs's locker is usually about 100 points luckier than Marty Barrett's locker. Similarly, some lockers are unluckier than others. Maybe the most unlucky locker in the major leagues is a large corner cubicle in the Baltimore Orioles' clubhouse. Don "Six Pack" Stanhouse used that locker for a season—then signed as a free agent with the Dodgers, where his career soon ended. The next resident was outfielder Dan Ford, who injured his knee and was forced to retire. The season after pitcher Steve Stone had won the AL's Cy Young Award he took the locker—and an elbow injury he suffered that season ended his career.

Eddie Murray took the locker next. If anybody could break the jinx it would be Eddie Murray, who had hit over .300 five times, had hit more than 30 home runs five times, and had knocked in more than 110 runs five times. That Eddie Murray. The same Eddie Murray, in fact, who hit .247 while playing for the Los Angeles Dodgers in 1989. After Murray abandoned the locker, veteran Rick Dempsey moved in. "I figured I could break the curse," he said. "I was in the locker for a year, and the Orioles tried to cut my salary 67 percent and I was gone." Dempsey hit .179 for the Dodgers in '89. Finally, Jim Traber occupied the locker in 1989. He hit .209, with 4 home runs.

The San Francisco Giants have a locker in their clubhouse that is gradually establishing its own reputation. Since 1988 four players have dressed in that locker: Phil Garner, who had it first, was given his unconditional release. Matt Williams, who had it next, was sent back to the minor leagues—although when he was recalled he took another locker and starred in the '89 playoffs. Tracy Jones, who inherited it, was traded from the pennant-winning Giants to the last-place Detroit Tigers, and Pat Sheridan, who took Jones's place on the roster and in the locker, hit .205, with 3 home runs, for the Giants.

Obviously, not all lockers are evil. In the town of Tidewater, Virginia, there was a cold, impersonal locker being used by Mets farmhand Mark Carreon. Carreon decided to make the locker a littler more friendly, so he bought what seemed like an ordinary gray throw rug and put it down in front of the cubicle. Strange things immediately began to happen.

Within a few days, Carreon was promoted to the New York Mets. He gave the carpet to infielder Keith Miller. Six days later Miller was recalled by the Mets. Miller gave the carpet to another infielder, Jeff McKnight. This was to be a real test of the powers of the carpet. "Things looked real slim for Jeff," Carreon said, and pretty slim for the growing reputation of the carpet. "He had never been on the major league roster. He'd never even been invited to spring training camp. And he'd sat on the bench in Tidewater the last two seasons."

Three weeks after receiving the carpet, Jeff McKnight was called up to the major leagues. The carpet was then presented to the outfielder Darren Reed. Reed hasn't been called up by the Mets...yet. But as Miller said, "That's the magic carpet ride to the majors."

Players are permitted to decorate their lockers any way they want to. Twins outfielder Dan Gladden hung the panic button switch right next to his locker. "That runs all the way to the front office," he informed reporters. "It's on 'off' right now, so you guys don't have to ask me if anybody is pushing the panic button, and we don't have to read any more about panicking. But you'd better keep your eyes on that switch."

The great sidearming relief pitcher Dan Quisenberry hung a sign over his locker reading: "Vietnam Veteran— We were winning when I left." The truth is that Quiz never served in Vietnam. "The rookies on the team saw the sign and started asking me questions about it," he explained, "so I just went along with them. I told them about being on reconnaissance missions in the Mekong Delta, hiding underwater for three hours, breathing out of a reed in my mouth. When they asked me about grenades, I told them I always threw overhand."

Braves outfielder Geronimo Berroa found a message in his locker one day. After dropping a routine fly ball in a game against the Pirates, he came into the clubhouse the next day to find a garbage pail hanging in his locker, with a note taped to it reading: "Try this."

And the Phillies' locker room just hasn't been the same

since Roger McDowell's pet snake, which lived in a box on top of McDowell's locker, died. Presumably of natural causes.

One of the oldest locker room traditions still in use is the "kangaroo court," which is usually convened after a team has won a ball game, and issues fines to players for doing things such as missing a sign, forgetting how many outs there are, giving up a hit to a batter after getting two strikes on him. When Sparky Lyle was judge of the Yankees' kangaroo court he used to impose a heavy fine on any player caught with an unattractive woman before midnight. "But after midnight there was no fine," he said.

Not every team has a kangaroo court. The '89 Yankees had one, and at the beginning of the season Tommy John was named judge. When someone asked pitcher Dave LaPoint why John had been chosen, LaPoint mentioned that John had been in the big leagues for twenty-five years, that he had won 286 games, and that he was well liked by his teammates. Then he told the truth: "He's the only one who looked like Judge Wapner."

In the Giants' kangaroo court, outfielder Brett Butler was fined for studying a shadow in the outfield—the shadow got a suspended sentence. And manager Roger Craig was fined for asking a cab driver for a receipt—after someone else had paid the fare.

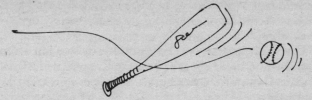

But When He's Good...

Most people march to the beat of their own drummer. Not Rickey Henderson. According to his agent, Richie Bry, Henderson "dances to his own drummer." As Rickey Henderson often says about himself, "I gotta be Rickey."

Henderson, who rarely reports to spring training the same day as his teammates, celebrated the opening of the 1989 season by not showing up for the opening day of training camp. New manager Dallas Green was visibly upset by Henderson's absence, saying, "I've been known to be understanding. I've been known to be gentle and kind. I'm not always the S.O.B. you reporters make me out to be. My wife likes me a lot."

To which Yankee PR director Harvey Green added, "But she's always reported on time."

When Henderson got off to a slow start with the Yankees, and his agent couldn't reach an agreement with the team on a new contract, the Yankees tried to trade him to San Francisco. Henderson exercised his right of refusal, canceling the deal. "I won't go to a team that's not a winner," he explained. The day he said that, the Giants were in first place in the NL West, 12 games above .500, while the Yankees were in second place in the AL East, a game below .500.

The situation in New York did not improve for Henderson. During a game against Kansas City he hit a ground ball past second base. The Royals' Frank White, then in the midst of establishing a consecutive-game errorless streak for second basemen, was given an error on the play. Henderson was so upset that he was not given a hit that he stood off the base staring up at the official scorer. And while he was busy staring, he was picked off first base.

After the game the official scorer changed his decision, giving Henderson a hit and keeping White's fielding streak alive. "I sure wish he would have done that before Rickey got picked off," Dallas Green said.

Henderson was finally traded to his hometown Oakland A's for a package of players that included young outfielder Luis Polonia. That gave Oakland a set of Hendersons—Rickey and Dave. "Just like Ozzie and Harriet," a local reporter pointed out.

When Polonia came to New York, he said, "I'm going to make people forget about Rickey Henderson, and I'm doing that right now. You don't hear people talk about him anymore. I'm young, I play for the team. I'm not a selfish player."

When Henderson was asked to respond to that quote, he laughed. "Luis Polonia make people forget about me? Tell him I'm a legend...He may have been misquoted, figuring it was New York and all. I mean, when people forget about me, baseball's over. I rewrote the book."

When he was reunited with his mother in Oakland, Henderson's bat came alive, and he helped lead the A's to the division title, American League Pennant, and World Championship. Asked by a reporter why he had suddenly started hitting when he got to Oakland, he explained, "My mother called me up to tell me what I was doing wrong."

Rickey was voted the Most Valuable Player in the playoffs, hitting .400 with 6 hits and 2 home runs, scoring 8 runs and compiling an incredible .609 on-base percentage. "Rickey is the man of the hour," pitcher Dave Stewart said, then added, "whatever the hour."

Delighting in the publicity, Rickey told reporters, "People said I didn't care when we lost. I did. If I didn't, I might as well have done what I wanted to do before my momma said no."

A reporter asked him exactly what that was.

"Play football," Henderson answered. "If she had let me go to college, I could have become Bo Jackson before Bo Jackson."

If Henderson ever manages to overcome his inferiority complex, he's going to be some player.

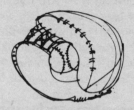

A Pitch in Time Often Saves the Nine

A wise old catcher once claimed, "Baseball is 75 percent pitching and 50 percent hitting." Obviously, that's not right. It's also at least 25 percent defense. But pitching is the key to winning in baseball. The Yankees, for example, had the fourth-highest hitting club in the big leagues—but also the second-to-worst pitching staff, and were out of contention by August.

Pitching has been described as an art, a science, and a mystery. Some pitchers with incredible ability never win in the major leagues, while others who look as if they should be pitching in Little League win consistently. The greatest strikeout pitcher of all time, Nolan Ryan, has lasted more than twenty big league seasons and became the first pitcher to strike out more than 5,000 batters—yet his record is barely above .500. As Cleveland's Bud Black said after losing a three-hitter to Cleveland, 1–0, "That's part of the game. Pitch good and you lose. Pitch bad and you win."

And every season a pitcher who has been very ordinary for several seasons suddenly emerges as a star. In 1989 that pitcher was the Cubs' Mike Bielecki. A very average pitcher for parts of several big league seasons, he was 18–7 in pitching the Cubs to the NL Eastern Division Title. "I know just when the transformation took place," he said. "It was in Caracas in the winter of 1988. The crowd was throwing stuff on the field. I was just trying not to get hurt. Believe me, when the fireworks are shooting past your head, you don't think too much out there, you just want to get three outs and get back to the dugout. That made me a much better pitcher."

It's a shame he didn't pitch during World War II. He could have been a Hall of Famer.

Mike Scott had been an average pitcher for several seasons before learning how to throw the split-fingered fastball and becoming one of baseball's best pitchers. But he's never forgotten how he had to struggle just to stay in the big leagues. After winning three games in six days during the '89 season, he said, "Back in my other life, before I was Mike Scott, it would have taken me parts of two seasons to get three wins."

Oakland's Todd Burns was another pitcher who came into his own in '89. "Pitching is pitching," he said confidently. "I'll take any and all I can get." And then he added, "Just don't wake me up."

Probably the pitcher who had the toughest luck in '89 was Toronto's Dave Stieb. It wasn't really unexpected.

In both of his last two starts in 1988, he was within one strike of a no-hitter when the batter got a hit. Although he pitched well in '89, compiling a 17—8 record and 3.35 ERA, he's still looking for the first no-hitter of his career. After throwing two more one-hitters in '89, he has five for his career. But the closest he came in '89 wasn't one of them. Pitching against the Yankees, he had a perfect game going with two outs in the ninth. He was one out away from perfection. Then New York's Roberto Kelly lined a 2—0 pitch for a double. Steve Sax followed with a hit to deprive Stieb of the one-hitter that would have given him six.

Later in the season, Stieb pitched one-hitters to beat Detroit and Milwaukee, but in both of those games he surrendered the only hit in the sixth inning. "I was relieved to give up that hit," he said after beating the Tigers. "After what happened last year, that's not something I want to go through unless I have a big lead. It's too painstaking having 1—0 and 2—0 leads with a no-hitter going."

Of course, it's often been said that one person's pain is another person's pleasure.

The only hit he gave up to the Brewers was an infield single that third baseman Kelly Gruber managed to knock down, but couldn't recover in time to make a play. "That ball hit me in the mitt," Gruber complained after the game. "It was a tough play, but I should have made it. It's tough to give a player an error when he dives for the ball, but I'm a believer that anytime a ball hits you in the mitt, you should make the play."

The official scorer saw it differently. In a statement that should warm the heart of every man who was ever criticized for a scoring decision, he said firmly, "It is a hit, it was a hit, and will always remain a hit."

But don't be so ambivalent about it, Joe.

Stieb was not the only pitcher to be teased by history in '89. Cincinnati's Tom Browning threw the only perfect game in 1988, and in '89 he was within three outs of becoming the first pitcher in big league history to pitch two perfect games. The Phillies' Dickie Thon changed history with a double leading off the ninth inning. "I never anticipated doing it the first time," Browning said afterward, "so there's no way to anticipate doing it a second time."

Earlier in the '89 season Browning had a no-hitter broken up with one out in the ninth innning, but that game wasn't nearly as perfect.

At least Browning won his games. When Mark Langston was pitching for Seattle, he entered the ninth inning of a game against the Blue Jays without giving up a hit, and holding on to a 2–0 lead. The Blue Jays came back to get a hit, three runs, and a victory. "I was in a daze," Langston told reporters, "but I wasn't upset... I've never been in a no-hitter in the ninth before. It was a new experience for me." Then he shook his head and added, "But not a very good one."

The worst enemy of the no-hit pitcher in '89 was Toronto's Nelson Liriano. Twice in one week he broke up no-hitters in the ninth inning, one pitched by Nolan Ryan, the other by Kirk McCaskill. Ryan took it in stride—he's got more no-hitters than anyone in history, so he throws back one-hitters—but this was only the second one-hitter of McCaskill's career, and the first time he'd gone into the ninth with a chance for a no-hitter. McCaskill was a trifle more disappointed than Ryan the day after Liriano had broken up his gem, explaining, "My wife told me not to shave for a couple of days. She wants me to keep razor blades away from my throat."

There is another way to look at no-hitters, of course. For example, when Blue Jays pitcher Alex Sanchez walked the first batter he faced in his first start of the year, catcher Bob Brenly strolled out to the mound and said optimistically, "Hey, you got your first batter out of the way and you still have your no-hitter going."

But perhaps the two pitchers who had the most to be disappointed about in 1989 were Oakland's Dave Stewart and the Dodgers' Ramon Martinez. Stewart has won more games in the last three years than any pitcher in baseball; he's the only big leaguer to have won 20 or more games each of the last three seasons, yet he's never won the Cy Young Award, given annually to the best pitcher in baseball. The '89 Cy Young Award went to the Royals' Bret Saberhagen. In fact, this is probably one of the best things that's ever happened to Stewart. Quick: name the 1988 NL Cy Young Award winner. It's not that easy to do. But Stewart has gotten more publicity out of not winning the Cy Young Award than almost all of the players who have won it. If he can keep winning his 20 games, then not getting the award, he'll become a baseball legend. I'm actually sorry I didn't think of this before it happened to Stewart—I would have started my campaign to get the Nobel Peace Prize years ago.

Actually, Stewart is very philosophical about the whole thing. "Nobody can take my three twenties away from me," he says. "I don't mind being known for them." Probably because he came very close to never getting them—when he was given his unconditional release by the Phillies early in the 1986 season, his lifetime record was 30–35.

The Dodgers' Martinez is at the very beginning of his career. After Los Angeles had played several extra-inning games and found themselves short of pitching, they recalled him from the minor leagues. Martinez took advantage of the opportunity, shutting out Atlanta on six hits. The Dodgers were so happy with his performance that they immediately sent him right back to the minor leagues.

It's probably a good thing he didn't pitch a no-hitter. What would they have done, released him?

But maybe the best-pitched game of the entire 1989 season took place in late August when, for the first time in big league history, two defending Cy Young Award winners faced each other. The unique confrontation between the NL's '88 winner, Orel Hershiser of the Dodgers, and Frankie Viola, who won the AL award with the Twins, came about after Viola had been traded to the Mets. Not only were these the defending Cy Young winners, they were also the two highest-paid pitchers in baseball. Usually, when there's so much expectation, these games turn out to be 11–10 cliff-hangers. But this game was every bit as good as its billing.

Of course, it didn't hurt that each pitcher was facing a lousy-hitting team. These were two of the worst-hitting clubs in baseball—the Mets ranked 19th in hitting, the Dodgers 24th. Viola won both the battle and the war, giving up only three hits and no walks, compared to Hershiser's eight hits and a walk, as the Mets clobbered the Dodgers, 1–0. Believe me, with these two teams, and these two pitchers, that's a clobbering.

"I can tell you one thing," Hershiser said after the game, "I'm not going to play in his charity golf tournament this winter. He's going to have to play in mine."

And Viola said with great satisfaction, "That was baseball at its best."

One pitcher who had absolutely nothing to be disappointed about this year was the Yankees' Andy Hawkins. Before the season started, his teammate on both the Padres and Yankees, Lance McCullers, said, "He [Hawkins] just wants to be another pitcher. He doesn't want to be known as a superstar."

Hawkins's wish came true, as he finished with a 15–15 record and 4.80 ERA. "I was two or three starts away from having a good year," he said in September. "But now I face a mediocre year. I can get 15 wins; that's not bad for a team 15 games under .500. But look at it the other way. I have 15 losses, and so that's not a good year. But it was close to a good year."

For every brilliant game pitched there are many more blowouts. So for most pitchers, the only thing as important as a live fastball or a sharp-breaking curveball is a good sense of humor. For example, Milwaukee Brewers pitcher Mark Knudson came in to relieve against the Mariners with two runners on base. After retiring the first batter he faced, he intentionally walked Alvin Davis to load the bases. Then he threw two consecutive wild pitches—the first one bounced so far away from the catcher that two runners scored, and the third runner scored on the second one. After that, manager Tom Trebelhorn walked out to the mound and told Knudson, "Well, that's one way to pitch out of a bases-loaded jam."

Veteran Charlie Hough, who lives and loses by his knuckleball, had a 10–13 season. Not only did he lose a one-hitter, one night against Cleveland he pitched 7⅔ innings and gave up only five hits—unfortunately, all of them were home runs. That came within one home run of tying the forty-nine-year-old record for home runs given up by one pitcher in one game. Earlier in the season Hough and the Yankees Dave LaPoint were locked up in a real hitter's battle—the hitters were fighting each other to get up to the plate against both of them. The Yankees finally won, 11–7. In a brief ceremony before the game started, First Lady Barbara Bush had thrown out the first ball, causing LaPoint to comment afterward, "She had better stuff than me or Charlie."

Seattle's Steve Trout never regained the pitching ability he had once shown with the White Sox, and was released before the end of the season. Trout pitched 30 innings in '89, giving up 43 hits, 17 walks, and 27 runs. The left-hander gave up 4 hits and a sacrifice fly to the last five left-handed batters he faced before being let go. Trout was actually quite open about his failures, admitting, "The last couple of outings have been a bit of a problem for me."

Another veteran, the Padres' Walt Terrell, also had a bad year. Unfortunately, his 5−13 record came in the last year of his contract. "You have to win more than five games in your free agent year," he said, "otherwise you can't expect a lot of teams to call." Then, after pausing, he added optimistically, "Except maybe some softball teams."

The day after making this statement Terrell was traded to the Yankees.

Veteran "Oil Can" Boyd had an injury-plagued year for the Red Sox, missing a large part of the season with a blood-clotting problem that threatened his career. Maybe that was why, after his first two starts, his ERA was a robust 11.25. When asked about his pitching problems, the usually talkative Boyd said, "I ain't doing no talking. I ain't doing no rapping."

In baseball, this is known as not taking the rap.

The Tigers' Jack Morris, who won more games in the 1980s than any pitcher in baseball, also had a rocky season. "His only luck this year has been bad," manager Sparky Anderson said. In May, after having beaten the Indians fifteen straight times in Tiger Stadium, he surrendered four home runs in three innings as Cleveland beat him in Detroit for the first time in his career, 7−3. I guess Morris took that as a pretty strong hint: the next day he went on the disabled list for the first time.

The Yankees' Dave LaPoint was another veteran who spent a lot of time on the disabled list in '89. LaPoint was pitching so poorly that when he was disabled hitters from every team in the league sent him "Get Well Soon" cards. Things started to go bad for him in spring training. After a long four-and-a-half-hour bus ride for a game with Montreal, LaPoint gave up 10 runs on 12 hits in only 4⅓ innings. "They've always hit me well," he said after the game, "and with me not having my good stuff today..." He shook his head and concluded, "That's a very bad combination."

Ken Phelps offered an excuse for LaPoint's performance, citing, "Bus lag."

There are some days when a pitcher doesn't have anything. In those situations there's little he can do except hope they haven't run out of hot water in the shower room. After Twins pitcher Roy Smith gave up hits to the first five Rangers he faced, for example, he was yanked. "I threw strikes," he said. "They just never reached the catcher's glove."

Former Boston star Bruce Hurst was bombed for 10 hits and 8 runs in only 5 innings when he made his National League debut with San Diego. "My target area was the dugout," he admitted. "The way I pitched, I could have gotten a hit off me. And I'm the world's worst hitter."

The Phillies' Ken Howell had a solid 12–12 season with the last-place team—except for the fact that he led the NL with 21 wild pitches, 7 more than his closest competitor—including 5 of them in one game. "I'm not a wild-pitch pitcher," he claimed. I don't know about that. A Detroit sportswriter figured out that 427 pitchers appeared in big league games in '88—and 382 of them threw 5 wild pitches or less for the entire season! Howell also arrived late at the ball park for the first game of a doubleheader, which he was supposed to pitch. "I knew

I was in trouble when I got out of my car and heard the national anthem."

A similar thing happened to the Yankees' Chuck Cary, who was caught in a traffic jam on the George Washington Bridge on a day he was supposed to pitch—and got out of his car and ran the final two miles to the ball park. "I ran for 15 minutes. When I got there, I was shaking like a leaf. I heard the national anthem playing and thought I'd missed it." The national anthem was playing, it turned out, at the beginning of the Old-Timers' Game. Cary pitched seven innings in the regular game, giving up only two hits. But afterward he decided, "Next time I'm supposed to start, I think I'll spend the night here."

One of the things I noticed in '89 was that pitchers rarely tried to make excuses for their own poor performances. For example, after getting hit hard two successive starts in Montreal's Olympic Stadium, Mark Langston said, "It's not the stadium's fault." And Toronto's Jimmy Key said, after getting off to a horrendous start and going on the disabled list, "In no way am I blaming my year on my arm."

I bet that made his leg nervous.

Without doubt, the longest trip to the mound in 1989 was taken by White Sox rookie Jose Segura. Segura flew into Chicago from Vancouver, home of the White Sox Triple A team, to pitch against the Cubs in an exhibition game. After that game Segura flew to Denver to meet his minor league team—but when he arrived in Denver he was told to fly right back to Chicago because he'd been officially recalled. He arrived in Chicago in time to appear in two ball games—giving up 8 earned runs in only 1⅓ innings. The Sox immediately sent him back to Denver to meet Vancouver. So in five days he piled up 11,139 air miles, or approximately 1,392 miles per earned run.

And how did you spend your weekend?

But probably the worst pitching record in organized baseball was compiled by the Dodgers' 1988 number one draft choice, Bill Bene. Bene started the season in Class A with Bakersfield, but was demoted to a rookie league. He threw a total of 16⅓ innings, giving up 17 hits and 36 walks. He hit 4 batters and threw 10 wild pitches, giving up 19 earned runs.

I don't know his earned run average. I've said I wasn't very good at higher mathematics.

Although Bene was not quoted on his performance, I suspect that the words of Kevin Appier, who pitched briefly and very ineffectively for the Royals before being sent back to the minors, might apply. "Things just started to snowplow," Appier said.

Probably the biggest change in baseball in the 1980s was the emergence of the bullpen as a key element in the success of a team. Once starting pitchers were expected to pitch as many as eight innings, and on occasion they would even do something once known as "pitching a complete game." That meant they pitched nine innings. Today a manager tells a starting pitcher, "Just give me six good innings." I never thought six innings was a lot. Gee, in every game I umpired, I always figured I had at least six good innings. And if that was good enough for a starting pitcher, why was everybody yelling at me?

Today at least half of every pitching staff is comprised of relief pitchers. The stopper, the short man, has become one of baseball's most glamorous players, maybe because the game is often on the line when he comes in to pitch. One of the things that has always made me laugh is watching a team struggle for eight innings, sweating in the heat, filthy from sliding in the dirt, and then, in the ninth, the bullpen gate opens and the stopper strides into the game in his sparkling clean uniform. He faces two batters: one of them flies out to the wall in dead center field, 410 feet away; the other one is robbed of a hit on a great play by the second baseman, who scrambles to his feet and just manages to throw out the batter to end the game—and everybody runs to the mound to congratulate the stopper!

Of course, that's only when he stops. Sometimes, maybe too often, the stopper leaks, and he gives up the hits that tie or lose the game. Supposedly, the thing that makes a great stopper is the ability to forget all about a bad performance and come right back the next day. But as the Yankees' stopper Dave Righetti says, "Until you die, you don't put them behind you."

Righetti knows that the one thing a relief pitcher simply can't afford to do—unless it's Mitch Williams—is walk a batter. "You just can't walk him," he says, "You walk a guy, the baseball gods score him."

I think Montreal's Andy McGaffigan best explained how a relief pitcher feels when he's come into a game and failed. "It's kind of frustrating," he says, "kind of like running over your own dog."

Two of the greatest relief pitchers of the 1980s were Dan Quisenberry and Kent Tekulve. Quiz, still pitching well for the Cardinals after a brilliant career in Kansas City, describes himself as "a garbage man. I come in and clean up other people's messes." Throughout his career Quiz has relied on excellent control, a great sinker, and a good defense. He's never struck out a lot of batters. But in one '89 performance he actually struck out the side. Naturally, he was quite modest about it. "That's the first time I've struck out the side since I don't remember when," he said after the game. "Eighth grade, I think. We were playing Whiffle ball. There was one seven-year-old kid. We were using his house, so he had to play."

Nineteen eighty-nine was a lot tougher for the 6'4",

190-pound Tekulve, whom Pete Rose described as "looking like a professional blood donor." Tekulve, who relieved in more games than any pitcher in history, was being used as a mop-up man by the Reds. After he'd pitched in 16 straight games that Cincinnati eventually lost, Pete Rose finally let him pitch in a game that the Reds won. "I've always done what's best for my club," Tekulve said after that game, "and right now, pitching once a week and getting beat is best for the club."

But finally the proud Tekulve couldn't take it anymore, and he retired in mid-season, explaining, "After all those years of being in the middle of things, I wasn't enjoying being on the fringe."

Another once fine reliever who retired in 1989 was the Red Sox' Bob Stanley. After being hit hard in several appearances, Stanley knew the end of his career was near, saying, "It's like a racehorse. Maybe it's time to go to the farm when you can't run anymore. That's how I feel."

Relief pitchers tend to be much more streaky than starters. Much like batters, they'll suddenly go into a slump for several games, during which time they can't get anybody out—even batters in slumps—and then, just as suddenly, they become unhittable. Braves reliever Joe Boever thought his slump, during which he lost five straight games, was caused because he failed to send out 20 copies of a chain letter he'd received. He decided he'd better do something about that. "I'm sending out 20 copies of the letter by Federal Express," he said after the fifth loss. "It'll cost me a thousand dollars, but it's worth it."

High on the list of worst relief performances turned in during the '89 season was Baltimore's Mark Williamson's appearance against Oakland. Williamson, who had a very good year, winning 10 games and compiling a fine 2.95 ERA, managed to achieve one of the rarest feats in relief pitching when he threw for the cycle, facing five batters and giving up a single, double, triple, and home run.

Maybe the Most Embarrassing Relief Appearance of 1989 never happened. In the first inning of a game against the Reds, Mets Pitcher Sid Fernandez was struggling, so manager Davey Johnson called his bullpen to order Rick Aguilera to get up. But at the time, Aguilera was busy answering Mother Nature's call. If he had gotten up, that would have been the sports story of the year. So the Mets, literally caught with their pants down, had to stay with Fernandez—who got the batter to hit into a double play. And everybody was relieved. Including Aguilera.

Maybe because of the constant mental pressure, relief pitchers tend to be a little stranger than starting pitchers. Their highs seem higher and their lows...also seem higher. Ranking alongside Mitch Williams in the character department is Cincinnati's fireballing reliever Rob Dibble. Dibble, who struck out 141 batters in only 99 innings, lives by the philosophy, "Everybody loses once in a while. If you could win every game, they couldn't pay you enough money." Nineteen eighty-nine was a very exciting season for him: he was fined by the team twice, once for missing a sign and once, in spring training, for throwing the clubhouse furniture into a lake, and he was suspended three times, although one of the suspensions was revoked after he appealed. His most publicized brush with the league law took place after the Cardinals' Terry Pendleton had singled in a run off him. Dibble very calmly walked toward the plate, picked up Pendleton's bat—and threw it as far as he could. It landed halfway up the screen behind home plate. "Sometimes," he admitted, "the frustration does get to you."

He was also suspended by the league for hitting the Mets' Tim Teufel with a pitch, and was suspended—but had it rescinded—after being quoted as saying he threw

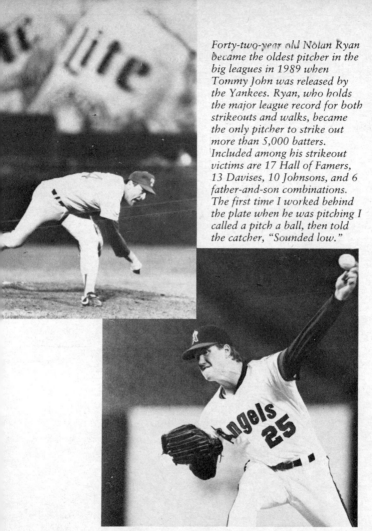

Forty-two-year old Nolan Ryan became the oldest pitcher in the big leagues in 1989 when Tommy John was released by the Yankees. Ryan, who holds the major league record for both strikeouts and walks, became the only pitcher to strike out more than 5,000 batters. Included among his strikeout victims are 17 Hall of Famers, 13 Davises, 10 Johnsons, and 6 father-and-son combinations. The first time I worked behind the plate when he was pitching I called a pitch a ball, then told the catcher, "Sounded low."

Among the best baseball stories of 1989 was the success of Angels rookie pitcher Jim Abbott, who overcame the handicap of being born without a right hand to make the big leagues. Abbott often had to answer monumentally stupid questions like, "If you had both hands, would you still be left-handed?" but managed to compile a 12–12 record. His 12 wins were the most games ever won in the big leagues by a player in his first year of professional baseball.

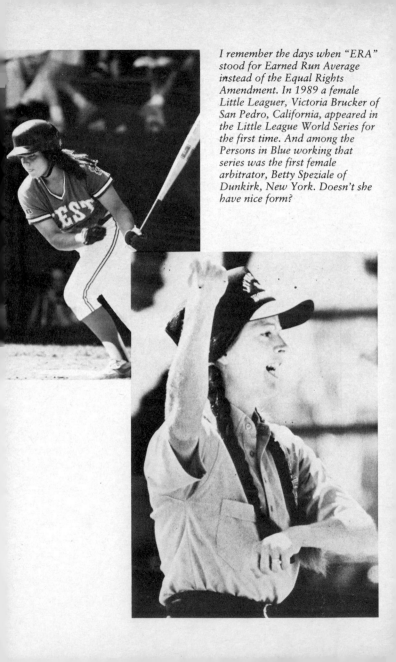

I remember the days when "ERA" stood for Earned Run Average instead of the Equal Rights Amendment. In 1989 a female Little Leaguer, Victoria Brucker of San Pedro, California, appeared in the Little League World Series for the first time. And among the Persons in Blue working that series was the first female arbitrator, Betty Speziale of Dunkirk, New York. Doesn't she have nice form?

Would I write a book without including a photograph of my friend Kenny Kaiser? Would George Steinbrenner keep a young pitcher? Would Pete Rose bet on baseball? Well, one out of three isn't bad. Here Kaiser demonstrates his famous one-legged balancing act, as a terrified inflatable hand signals him to stop.

The 1989 World Series really was the Fall Classic—or maybe the Fault Classic. The Series between the Giants and A's was suspended for more than a week after a major earthquake took place along the San Andreas Fault. Here Giants pitcher Steve Bedrosian models a new cap that might be worn by people who don't have no-fault insurance, in case something else were to fall during the Classic.

When the Mets went to spring training last year, manager Davey Johnson was determined to find a way for his pitchers to hold runners on base. Here Lenny Dykstra and Mookie Wilson wonder why it's called spring training instead of elastic training.

Among the finalists for baseball's 1989 Best Dressed List was that Giant of fashion, that hombre of habiliment, that señor of sartorial splendor Rick Reuschel. Unfortunately, in a very close vote, Reuschel finished 632nd.

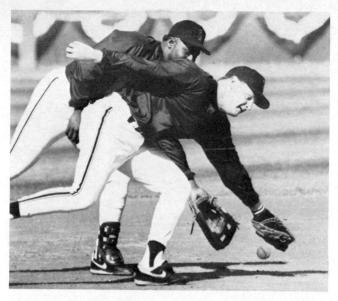

The year 1989 also saw the introduction of the popular new Olympic event Synchronized Baseball. (Above) Giants Matt Williams and Kevin Mitchell rehearse their routine, which, as seen (below), seems to still need some work.

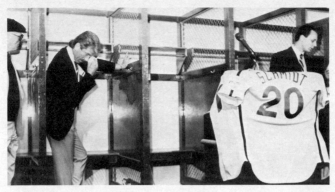

Among the stars who retired from baseball in 1989 were Yogi Berra, Steve Carlton, Bob Horner, Kent Tekulve, Bruce Sutter, Bob Stanley, and, pictured here, Mike Schmidt. "I had a handful of times nobody had," Schmidt said during his tearful announcement. "My flame just went out."

This is your fill-in-the-caption exercise. Obviously, I could write something hysterically funny about the way the Cubs' Jerome Walton is sliding into the Mets' Kevin Elster. I could also cause this book to be banned in several states by doing so. I could also cut off my nose to spite my face, but with my nose, my face would think it was an improvement.

I know what you're thinking: Ah ha! The truth is finally revealed. Umpires do wear glasses. Wrong. Maybe it looks as if Frank Pulli is cleaning his glasses, but he's really searching for Tommy Lasorda, who was seen wearing these glasses just before he went on his diet.

The 1989 Montreal Expos thought the NL Eastern Division title was in the bag; unfortunately for them, it just turned out to be pitcher Pascual Perez. A very loyal player, here Perez is just trying to Expos his new haircut—but it makes me worry about what he's going to do in 1990 when he realizes he's playing for the Yankees.

BO JACKSON

BLACK &

KIRBY PUCKETT

PUCKET
WRECKING C
"NO WALL IS TOO TA

34

THE WRECKING BALL

Posters have become very popular collectible items. Here Bo Jackson poses in front of a locker half-filled with baseball equipment and half-filled with football equipment, and Kirby Puckett poses at a construction site. I was once asked to pose for a poster, too. They explained I was going to be the "Before" in a "Before-and-After" series. I asked them, "Before what?" and they told me, "Everything."

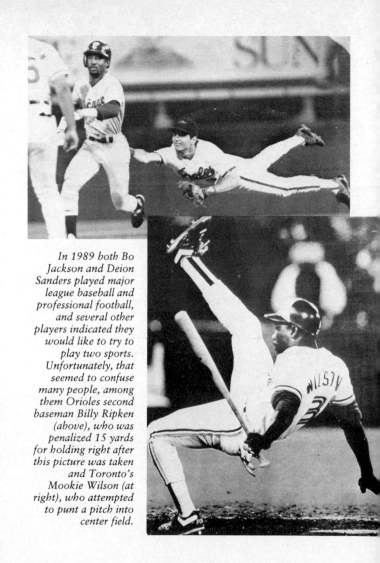

In 1989 both Bo Jackson and Deion Sanders played major league baseball and professional football, and several other players indicated they would like to try to play two sports. Unfortunately, that seemed to confuse many people, among them Orioles second baseman Billy Ripken (above), who was penalized 15 yards for holding right after this picture was taken and Toronto's Mookie Wilson (at right), who attempted to punt a pitch into center field.

*A rare Canadian gorilla, wearing a popular "Silly Fan Mask,"
celebrates the opening of Toronto's Skydome indoor-outdoor
stadium. On opening day Blue Jays officials discovered they'd sold 79
tickets for seats that didn't exist. The third game played in the
Skydome had to be halted during a rainstorm because it took too
long to get the roof closed. I once had a convertible with the same
problem.*

*Former President Ronald Reagan, who started his show business
career as a broadcaster doing re-creations of Cub games, worked the
first inning of the All-Star Game with Vin Scully. Offering insights
like, "Tony Gwynn played basketball in college," Reagan again
proved how smart he was to take the job of President rather than
holding out for a network broadcasting slot.*

One of the most difficult things a big leaguer must do is keep up with the latest congratulatory handshake. The "high fives" and "low fives" of the early eighties are now officially extinct, as is the "Elbow Bash" popularized by the A's "Bash Brothers." Now officially in is the "Death Grip" demonstrated here by A's Tony Phillips and Mark McGwire.

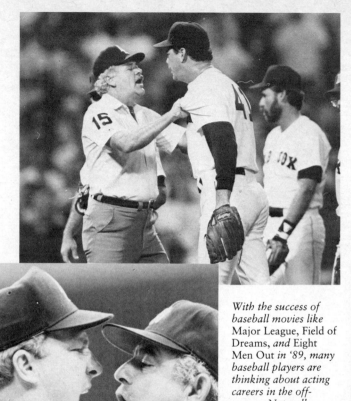

With the success of baseball movies like Major League, Field of Dreams, *and* Eight Men Out *in '89, many baseball players are thinking about acting careers in the off-season. Naturally, umpires are willing to offer helpful hints. Here, for example, (at left) Joe Brinkman works with Mike Smithson between innings on a scene from* A Streetcar Named Desire, *and (below) Larry Young tutors coach Lee Elia on a scene from* Rambo III.

National League participants in baseball's 1989 All-Star Dance Party contest are (counterclockwise from right) Kevin Mitchell, Howard Johnson, Glenn Davis, and Eric Davis in a traditional square dance. Although the NL won the dance segment of the evening's competition, the AL won the baseball game, 5–3.

After compiling the highest ERA of any pitcher who threw enough innings to qualify for the ERA title in '88, the Angels' Bert Blyleven said, "I've been reading things like, 'He's done. He's over the hill. He'll be lucky to make the staff . . .' When you hear things like that it motivates you. You want to go out there and punch people in the face." Or at least stick your tongue out at them. Blyleven came back with a tremendous 17–5 record and 2.73 ERA, fourth best in the league.

Among my many official duties in 1989 was to serve as spokesperson and official umpire for Fisher Nuts' "Sports Nut of the Year" contest. The winner of this national search for America's nuttiest sports fan was J. Duffy Dwyer, a.k.a. the "Phantom Friar," who claims he never misses a Providence College game. Here he is being crowned with the official Fisher Nuts Bucket of Peanuts, an honor so great that even people like Henry Kissinger, Queen Elizabeth, Dustin Hoffman, and Mother Teresa have not even been nominated.

The five major sets of baseball cards issued in 1989 were Topps, Fleer, Score, Donruss, and Upper Deck. The Most Valuable Card in '89 was Upper Deck's Ken Griffey, Jr., card, which is valued at $15.

Most basebrawls consist of pushing, shoving, and threatening, as in this fight between Montreal and Houston. After a fight between California and the White Sox, for example, Angels pitcher Bob McClure said, "I got a couple of knocks on my head. My kids do worse than that." Oakland's Mark McGwire advises, "It doesn't pay to get on the bottom of the pile in a fight. You can't do anything, and you're eating grass the whole time." In one fight where some damage might have been done, the Dodgers' Kirk Gibson went after Montreal's Pascual Perez, but before Gibson could reach him, he was tackled by the Expos' Kevin Gross. Afterward Gross claimed, "I got my first save of the year tonight."

at Willie Randolph. After his wild season, Dibble still believes people really don't understand him. "People think I'm a big jerk," he said, "but people don't know the way I am. They don't see me go to mass every Sunday. They just see me on the field."

Later, he added, "Being Hungarian, sometimes I lose my mind. People must wonder if I'm a lunatic. I'm not as crazy as I appear to be, but sometimes I can't help the way I act."

On the other side of the brain there is the Dodger rookie who appeared mostly in relief, John Wetteland. Wetteland, the son of a jazz musician, doesn't watch TV or go to the movies; instead he writes poetry and plays the piano. "In my spare time," he explained to a reporter, "I enjoy serving doughnuts on another planet."

Wetteland might be the only relief pitcher in history who works on his poetry in the bullpen. "We have contests out there where you have to name five poets," he says, "any five poets. I'm excluded from those contests."

"He'll come running through the living room in the middle of the day," explains bullpen catcher Todd Maulding, who rents Wetteland a room in his house, "and he'll be in the middle of a 'Skies Are Blue...' rap. The man doesn't care what anybody thinks about him." Then Maulding adds with great respect, "He knows words nobody knows. Man knows real words."

Wetteland would probably get along well with Houston's Larry Andersen, who in addition to worrying about why we park on the driveway and drive on the parkway, wonders, "What does God say when he sneezes?" and "Is Robin Hood's mother called motherhood?" Andersen's own philosophy of life is very simple, "You can only be young once, but you can be immature forever."

Another one of the nicest stories of the 1989 season was the comeback of Orioles relief pitcher Kevin Hickey.

In the late 1970s, twenty-one-year-old Kevin Hickey was laid off by the mill in which he was working. With nothing else to do while he searched for another job, he started playing semipro baseball. His fastball attracted the attention of several scouts, who asked him to throw a curveball. "Well," he admitted, "I know what one is, but I don't know how to throw it."

He learned quickly, though, and signed with the White Sox. "They gave me $500 and a book called *How to Speak Hillbilly* and sent me to Paintsville, Kentucky. That's not too far from Swamp Branch and Flatgap." Within three years he was pitching for the Sox, appearing in 101 games in relief in 1981 and 1982. At the end of the '82 season he hurt his arm and was eventually released. Through the rest of the 80s he was signed—and released—by the Yankees, Phillies, White Sox (again), and Giants. When no major league team wanted him, he pitched in the minors for Denver, Columbus, Albany, Reading, Portland, Honolulu, and Phoenix. "If they gave out frequent flyer mileage in the minors," he says, "right now I could be flying around the world."

By 1988 he was so broke he was living in a minor league locker room and waiting tables in Mike Ditka's Chicago restaurant. But then, just as suddenly as his arm had started hurting seven years earlier, it stopped. At age thirty-three, he pitched his way onto the Orioles' staff, appearing in 51 games, with a 2.92 ERA. "It could be a movie, couldn't it?" Hickey says of his career. "They haven't invented a word to say how excited I am to be back in the majors... Dorothy said there's no place like home, and she was right. As a matter of fact, if I could, I'd wear velvet cleats and click my heels three times."

Or maybe he should just call Wetteland and get one of his words.

Another former major leaguer who attempted to make a comeback in 1989 was Pete Falcone, who last pitched in the big leagues in 1984. After retiring with a 70–90 lifetime record, Falcone went into the home remodeling business, although he had always claimed his real goal was to own a Seven-11 convenience store. Some baseball writers assumed he wanted to do that because it reminded him of his ERA. Falcone was sorry he didn't open the store because his remodeling business failed and "guys who own those fast food places are loaded."

Instead, he pitched winter ball in the Dominican Republic in 1988 and showed enough to interest the Dodgers, who signed him to a minor league contract. After a brief stint with the Dodgers' Triple A team in Albuquerque, where he gave up 5 runs in 1⅓ innings, he was sent to San Antonio in the Double A Texas League, where he was 3–4 with a high ERA. Dodger general manager Fred Claire admits Falcone's chances are "one in a thousand…one in a million," but Falcone doesn't mind, explaining, "I know it's a long shot. I knew that. Even if I don't get there, I tried. It's a miracle I got this far. If I do make it, it'll be a great story.

Then he can sell the movie rights, and fulfill the dream of every major leaguer—open his own convenience store.

Pitchers, both starters and relievers, will do absolutely anything to win. I know this might shock you, but there are some pitchers who actually break the rules of baseball to gain an advantage. Sorry to break it to you like this. For years, for example, people have accused Houston's Mike Scott of defacing the ball—cutting the cover to make it drop suddenly. In '89 the Dodgers' Tommy Lasorda claimed he'd sent several balls scratched by Scott during the game to the National League office. "But I don't know what they do with them," he admitted. "Maybe they give them to their grandchildren."

After Scott had beaten the Dodgers for his twentieth victory of the '89 season, L.A. reliever Jay Howell showed reporters a ball that he claimed Scott had used in the game. "This is like a chainsaw massacre," he complained.

Phillies manager Nick Leyva says he caught Scott hiding a very small piece of sandpaper in his glove. "But," Leyva explained, "when the umpire went out to check Scott, Scott ate the sandpaper."

And I guess that's what pitchers refer to as a "rough outing."

Another pitcher accused of doctoring the baseball in '89 was Toronto's thirty-year-old reliever Frank Wills. After a long and undistinguished career, Wills finally earned a spot in the Blue Jays' bullpen after learning to throw the sinker he has nicknamed "Titanic." Batters agree that that name is appropriate, because it's so wet.

One of the pitchers most often accused of loading up a ball is Pascual Perez. Perez is one of baseball's most interesting characters. After striking out Mike Schmidt early in the '89 season, Perez was so happy he did a Michael Jackson moonwalk off the mound. During another game he faked a pick-off throw by pretending to throw between his legs. One day, after a routine putout at first base, instead of throwing the ball to the second baseman for a routine around-the-horn toss, he whipped it to centerfielder Otis Nixon. When Perez was accused of putting a foreign substance on the ball in 1989, Expos PR director Richard Griffin pointed out, "Pascual Perez is a foreign substance."

Other teams have frequently accused Perez of loading up a pitch or ten, sometimes claiming that he applies grease from his hair to the ball. "You can see him go to his hair and not wipe it on his jersey," the Reds Jeff Reed says. Umpires searched him several times during the '89 season, causing manager Buck Rodgers to say, "He'd better get used to it. It's obvious other teams are playing with his head." After Perez started the '89 season with an 0–6 mark, Rodgers added, "And so far it's working."

Perez, of course, denies everything. He claims the only trick pitch he throws is the blooper, which he tosses on a very high arc. "I can throw it for a strike anytime I want," he says. "In my country, they call it the 'Pascual Pitch.'"

But probably the most unusual pitch Perez made came during a game against the Cubs. Chicago's Jerome Walton hit a line drive that ricocheted off Perez's arm and was caught on a fly by second baseman Jeff Huson. Someone in the Cubs' dugout must have said something, because when Perez got the ball back, he suddenly spun around and whipped a strike into the Cubs' dugout. I think, in my country, *that's* what's called the "Pascual Pitch."

The Mets' Bob Ojeda claimed he threw a new pitch at least once in '89. After giving up a long home run to Mike Scioscia, he was asked what type of pitch Scioscia had hit. Ojeda thought about it a minute, then replied, "That was my I'm-getting-tired fastball."

Supposedly, the Montreal Expos have signed a sixteen-year-old pitcher from the Dominican Republic who has six fingers on each hand. One reporter said, "You've heard of a split-fingered fastball? This kid throws a six-fingered fastball." And another reporter added, "He's going to be twice as good as 'Three-Fingered' Brown."

The thing about pitching is that absolutely no one can predict how well any pitcher will do in any one game until the game starts. For example, Andy Hawkins faced nine Red Sox hitters one day, giving up eight runs and getting one out. "I'm sure he's pitched better at times during the year," manager Bucky Dent said afterward. But warming up in the bullpen before the game, Hawkins felt very confident. "He had great stuff out there," pitching coach Billy Connors said. "He had his best fastball in a long time. He felt great." And then Connors pointed out the only problem: "He just couldn't get anybody out."

The exact opposite thing happened to Boston's Mike Smithson. After shutting out the Indians on two hits, Smithson said, "Throwing on the side before the game, I was absolutely terrible. I had no idea where the ball was going. I had no slider. While I was warming up I told pitching coach Bill Fischer it would take a miracle for me to go more than two innings. I guess miracles do happen."

Pitchers can't hit—legally, in the American League, and physically, in the National League. The American League doesn't even waste time allowing them to try to hit. The National League still prefers to let let them go up to the plate and take a few silly swings or maybe bunt the ball and then go back to the dugout. In the National League, watching the pitcher strike out is called "tradition." As a former American Leaguer, naturally I prefer the designated hitter; in fact, I helped write the rule. I just don't think it adds excitement to the game watching a pitcher stand at the plate and try, most of all, not to get hurt.

National League pitchers take a lot of pride in their hitting ability, even though very few of them can hit well enough to succeed in the low minor leagues. Several veteran pitchers who spent their careers in the American League pitched in the National League this year and got to bat for the first time. When the Padres' Bruce Hurst got a hit in only his third major league at bat, he explained modestly, "Don't ask me how. Even a blind dog finds a bone every once in a while." Unfortunately, that was his only hit in his first 35 at bats—during which he added a tremendous amount of action to the game by striking out 28 times. "This is the worst slump of my career," he complained. "I don't know what it is. Maybe a lack of talent."

But finally he snapped his 0 for 32 streak with a single off the Cardinals' Jose DeLeon. "Nobody was more surprised about that than me," he confessed, then corrected himself, "except maybe DeLeon."

Frankie Viola was so thrilled when he got his first major league hit, a single off Orel Hershiser, that he asked Hershiser to autograph the ball.

Dan Quisenberry went 0 for 3 with the Cardinals after not batting once during his ten seasons in the AL. Quiz showed an unusual batting stance for a human being, lifting his leg into the air before he swung the bat. "Mel Ott did it and it worked for him," Quiz said. "I'm just not sure I'm lifting the right leg." After grounding out to second base, a chagrined Quiz had his excuse all ready: "I thought they were playing zone," he said, "but they were in man-to-man."

Obviously it was a good thing for some of these new National Leaguers that they didn't have to bat in the AL. Houston's Jim Clancy, for example, who'd spent twelve seasons with the Blue Jays, got on base for the first time in his career with a single—and was forced to leave the game when he pulled his hamstring muscle running to first base.

Probably the biggest surprise was the batting performance of Mark Langston, who banged out 4 hits in his first 15 at bats.

There are some pitchers who are pretty good hitters, among them the Cardinals' Joe Magrane. In the tenth inning of a game against the Pirates, Whitey Herzog sent Magrane up to pinch-hit with the bases loaded. "I didn't expect to get in until the twenty-seventh inning," Magrane admitted after the game. "All my batting equipment was packed up because the team was getting ready to leave for Pittsburgh right after the game, so I had to unpack it. I thought we'd get penalized for delay of game."

Magrane walked on six pitches, forcing in the go-ahead run. He never swung the bat. Actually, it wasn't too surprising that Whitey used Magrane as a pinch-hitter. The Cardinals' longest home run of the season was a 417-foot blast hit by pitcher Scott Terry.

Pascual Perez is not one of the pretty good hitters in the NL. In fact, going into the '89 season he had banged out only 30 hits in 288 exciting at bats. But after finishing a stay in a drug rehabilitation clinic, Perez went on a batting tear, getting 3 hits in his next 15 at bats. Unfortunately, at the same time, his pitching record was 0–6, forcing Expos PR Director Richard Griffin to announce, "We want to sign the batting coach at the rehab center, but not the pitching coach."

Some pitchers really shouldn't even pretend to try to hit. The most embarrassing moment of Pirate pitcher Bob Walk's big league career came, he said, "when I walked to the plate in Chicago without my bat."

And here is the Safe Offer of the Year Story: a Philadelphia charity volunteered to donate $100 to the ALS Foundation, which raises money to fight Lou Gehrig's disease, for every hit by Phillies pitcher Don Carman. I guess the added pressure was too much 'or Carman. A lifetime .046 hitter, with 8 hits in 174 at bats, he had only one bunt single in 34 thrilling at bats this season.

Just as pitchers get to bat, on occasion position players get to pitch. That usually happens when one team is so far in front of the other that anything short of a disaster like the return of Earl Weaver to the dugout isn't going to change the outcome, and the manager doesn't want to use a live pitcher in a game he considers lost. For example, Tommy Lasorda brought in utility man Mickey Hatcher to pitch the final inning of a game in which the Cardinals were blowing out the Dodgers, 12–0. The inning Hatcher pitched was the only inning that the Cardinals didn't get at least one hit. Actually, that's not true, there was one Cardinal hit—the first batter Hatcher faced. And after hitting him with a pitch, he balked, then walked three batters in a row to force in a run. And then he retired the side. Hatcher's best pitch...Hatcher's only pitch is a fastball...a straightball, which was timed on the radar gun at 82 mph. Of course, starting pitcher Fernando Valenzuela's fastball was clocked at only 81. Well, maybe that's the reason Hatcher was in the game in the first place. Meeting the media after the game, Hatcher said, "I needed one more inning. I was starting to find the strike zone." Then he sighed and added, "I wish I hadn't given up that run. We might have battled back and won."

Two position players pitched for the Astros when they were blown out by the Pirates, 17–5. It was actually the second career appearance on the mound for Greg Gross. In the two thirds of an inning he'd pitched previously, he struck out the two batters he faced. This time he gave up three hits and a walk, accounting for one earned run. After the game he admitted, "I think I'm losing something." Craig Reynolds also pitched an inning in the game, surrendering four runs, three earned, on three hits and a walk. Commenting on Reynolds's performance, Pirates pitching coach Ray Miller said professionally, "Obviously Reynolds doesn't pitch that well on a thousand days' rest."

Ranger shortstop Jeff Kunkel accomplished a rare feat for a position player when he hit a home run and gave up a home run in the same game. Kunkel had pitched one perfect inning in '88, so when the Twins were smashing the Rangers 14–3, Texas manager Bobby Valentine figured the time was right for Kunkel. Kunkel, who actually tried pitching in the Instructional League, came in with one out in the eighth and runners on second and third. He got out of that jam, giving up only one hit. But oh, that ninth. He walked the first two batters, then gave up a long home run to Randy Bush.

Probably the best performance by a pitching non-pitcher was turned in by the Brewers' Terry Francona, who hurled a perfect inning against the A's. He even managed to strike out Stan Javier on a beautiful knuckleball. After the game Javier said he was very impressed, claiming, "I thought that was Charlie Hough I was facing." Since Francona was hitting only .154 as a player, a reporter wondered if he'd ever considered making the transition to the mound. "Did you see my velocity out there?" Francona asked. "I don't want to pitch; I want to be a hitter." Then he pointed out the obvious, "But I'm not that, either."

One former position player who is attempting to make that transition is Terry Blocker, who was the Mets' No. 1 draft choice in 1981. Blocker, who pitched in the Braves' minor league system in '89, had a conversation about his chances with pitching coach Bruce Del Canton. "He told me my fastball had good movement and philosophy."

Later, someone told Blocker that Del Canton had said "good movement and velocity."

1989 Crime Report

Baseball players aren't immune to the same problems faced by all the non-major leaguers of the world. For example, returning to his house with his family late one night, Dodger Kirk Gibson was held up at gunpoint by a man who took his new BMW and several hundred dollars in cash. Wade Boggs, who had other problems, was threatened by a man who held a knife to his throat. "Get a knife stuck to your throat," Boggs suggested; "that puts a lot in perspective." Both Cardinal outfielder Pedro Guerrero and Dodger broadcaster Don Drysdale were robbed. A woman slipped Mickey Finns, a knockout pill, into their drinks, then robbed them while they were out. And finally, Toronto's Kevin Batiste was arrested for having a loaded handgun in the luggage he checked for an airplane flight. Although the gun had been reported stolen, Batiste was worried: "I don't want people thinking I stole that gun. It was given to me by a good friend. I was kind of using it for protection." I'll tell you, those luggage fleas better to be very careful.

And finally, then there's the case of Jose Canseco. But that's a longer story.

Gamblin' Rose

The Baseball Story of the Year took place off the field in 1989. Years from now baseball fans won't remember that the Baltimore Orioles made one of the greatest improvements in history, or that Kevin Mitchell had a career year to win the National League MVP or that one-handed pitcher Jim Abbott made his debut. What will be remembered is that Baseball Commissioner Bart Giamatti banished for life one of the greatest players in history, Pete Rose. Pete Rose, who holds the major league record for holding major league records, but is best known for getting more hits, 4,256, than anyone else, started the year as manager of the Cincinnati Reds. On February 20, retiring commissioner Peter Ueberroth asked Rose to come to his office for a meeting. "They wanted my input and advice on a couple of things," Rose said. "I gave it to them. It took an hour. I left." But slowly word leaked out: the Commissioner's office was investigating reports that Pete Rose had bet on baseball games. Under the rules of baseball, that is an infraction punishable by lifetime suspension.

When *Sports Illustrated* reported that Rose had bet on games, he denied it completely, saying, "I'd be willing to bet you, if I was a betting man, that I have never bet on baseball."

There wasn't too much doubt that he was a betting man. His former wife said he had once refused to pay a gambling debt and had received a dead fish in the mail.

The case dominated the sports pages for most of the baseball season. Eventually, a man convicted of tax fraud who was serving as a government informant, and an Ohio bookie awaiting sentencing on drug-trafficking and income tax evasion convictions offered to give evidence against Rose. The FBI announced it had found his fingerprints on betting slips. It was revealed that Rose had lost tens of thousands of dollars gambling, and he had sold many of the mementos he'd received during his career to cover his losses. And finally, Rose was accused of betting on Cincinnati Reds games.

Throughout the season Rose continued to deny that he had ever bet on baseball games. While being interviewed by the private investigator hired by the Commissioner's office, John Dowd, Rose admitted that he had gambled on other sports, something that is completely legal under baseball's rules. "I like to watch sports on TV," he said, "and I like to bet on them if I'm watching them... Hell, I've got a $25,000 television unit at home. I get everything. I get you walking through the airport when the monitor hits you."

"Is that right?" Dowd asked.

"Yes," Rose said, "I can get everything on the TV."

"So you're the one who puts those cameras on me, huh?"

"Yes. Don't carry no bombs aboard."

Dowd's 225-page report, with seven volumes of exhibits, was submitted to the Commissioner's office in early May. Later it was revealed that the report included testimony from several people who claimed to have knowledge of Rose's bets, including a bookie named Ron Peters, who said that Rose had won a total of $67,000 betting on baseball in May and June of 1987.

Upon receiving the report, Giamatti asked Rose to come to his office for a hearing. This gets a little complicated. A little? Trigonometry was easier. But at about this time Peters was due to be sentenced on the drug and tax charges and Giamatti wrote to the judge deciding on the sentence, saying that Peters "has been candid, forthright and truthful with my special counsel." Rose, after asking for, and receiving, a postponement of his hearing, filed suit in an Ohio court to block Giamatti from ruling on the whole matter, claiming that Giamatti's letter in Peters's behalf was proof that he had already made up his mind, and that Rose could not get a fair hearing. The court granted Rose his temporary injunction—and baseball spent the summer in court.

As the story unfolded, Rose tried to do his job as Reds manager, but wherever the team played, the media only wanted to talk to him about the case. Rose described the reporters and photographers who followed him as "me and my shadows. I feel like a fresh piece of meat." So many TV and photographers were constantly taking his pictures, he pointed out, "We know that Kodak's in good shape."

Meanwhile, he continued to insist that he wasn't worried about the outcome. "When you're doing nothing, why worry? People who do something worry. People that worry jump off bridges. I can walk across any bridge in the world."

The Rose case became one of the biggest news stories of the summer of '89, and it was almost impossible to open a magazine or turn on the TV news without seeing him. "I've been on the cover of *Sports Illustrated* three times since this investigation started," he said, "and I haven't gotten a hit...

"I'm on the cover of *Time*. It took me 4,256 hits to get in the cover of *Time*. It took me twenty-four years to get on the cover of *Time*. And all of a sudden, I'm accused of betting on baseball and I'm on the cover again…

"I've had friends call me and [tell me they'd] thought I'd died because they're sitting there watching Tom Brokaw on NBC News and all of a sudden my picture's up there. They hear him say, 'He may have managed his last game.' They say, 'What happened to him, his plane crash or something?'"

Pete Rose's personal life became fair game. Long stories were written about his relationship with his ex-wife, his children, other women. One of the men who claimed to have placed bets for Rose, Paul Jangzen, who had been convicted of income tax evasion, told of a trip they'd taken on which Rose brought along a girl he'd met a few weeks earlier. "I check into my room, they check into their room. These rooms are next to each other… A half hour after we're in the room there's a knock at the door." It was Rose's wife. "Pete is frantic. 'Paul, would you please take the blame. If I put the girl in your room, we'll lock the middle door. I'll tell my wife you're with the girl, then I'll…I'll be all right.'

"So he lets [his wife] in and they are arguing and fighting…and he finally throws her out of his room. I said 'Pete, I'll take this girl to the airport, just get in there with your wife…stay with her and I'll take the blame.'

"He says, 'Hell with that…I didn't drive two hundred miles to sleep with my wife.'"

Baseball fans were divided on their opinion about the situation. When the Reds returned to Cincinnati for Opening Day, Rose was greeted with signs of support reading "We Bet We Back Pete," and "Pete Will Come Out Smelling Like a Rose." A billboard in downtown Cincinnati simply carried the message "Say It Ain't So, Bart." A Dayton, Ohio, car wash took an unofficial poll, allowing customers to have their car washed "For Pete,"

"Against Pete," or "Undecided." People who came clean were roughly evenly divided, with undecideds trailing slightly.

One of Pete's biggest supporters was Morganna, the sporting world's lavishly endowed "Kissing Bandit," who was known for running onto the field to kiss stars. She claimed that Pete Rose had been the first pro athlete she'd ever kissed on the field. "That was in 1971, and Pete Rose has been my friend ever since," she said. "We've gotten together a few times. He was my first kiss and he'll always be special to me. It absolutely tears my heart out to see what he's going through now. Besides, my uncle was a bookie and he was always nice too."

Maybe his most unusual support came from former teammate Bernie Carbo who found it hard to believe that Rose would have bet as much as he was accused of betting. "The man was so cheap," he said. "When I joined the Reds in 1970 we had a team meeting where we decided to pool the money we received from doing pregame and postgame radio shows and use it to throw parties at the All-Star break at the end of the year.

"Rose stood up and said, 'I'm going to be the star of the game the majority of the times, so why should I pay for the party?' and walked out of the room.

"Whenever he was named star of the game after that, we'd take a roll of pennies and break it open in his locker. There'd be pennies everywhere.

"So what did Pete do? He went out and bought himself a big ol' piggy bank. By the end of the season it was filled."

Rose's whole family got involved. His son, Pete Jr., playing his first season of pro baseball in the Orioles' minor league system, struggled at bat and was often heckled by opposing fans. People would wave dollar bills at

him and shout things like, "You got a bet on the game?"
Once Pete Jr.'s mother confronted a particular obnox-
ious fan who asked her if she had a problem. "No," she
said, "you got the problem because that's my son and
you're either going to hit the pavement or take your best
shot at me."

Pete's own mother, living in Cincinnati, said she's
stopped watching television because of the scandal and
didn't attend a single Reds game. A reporter visiting her
home asked her why there wasn't a single picture of her
son hanging on the walls. "I don't need pictures," she
said, smiling, "I know what the brat looks like."

The Pete Rose Case became the subject of jokes,
poetry, even songs. Comedian Jay Leno said, "A new sur-
vey shows that Americans have lost confidence in savings
and loans. Sixty-three percent would rather have Pete
Rose handle their money."

An Orioles fan named Tom Weeks won the honor of
throwing out the first ball at an O's game by claiming to
be so loyal that "I'll always be there to root, root, for the
home team, the Baltimore O's; I'm picking them for first
this year, it's no gamble, I've consulted Pete Rose."

Mark Bradford, who composes musical spoofs,
teamed with lyricist Jerry Thomas, a Cincinnati disc joc-
key to write the song "Gamblin' Rose," which actually
became a minor hit. Set to the tune of the 1962 Nat King
Cole hit "Ramblin' Rose," it went:

> Gamblin' Rose, Gamblin' Rose, why you gamble,
>   no one knows.
> With no bets down, you are all frowns, what a
>   letdown, you Gamblin' Rose.
>
> Where's your bat, where's your car? Did you lose
>   them in some bar?

Charlie Hustle's days are numbered, and the odds
   are long and far.

Marge Schott says, "Just play ball," Ueberroth just
   hit the wall.
For your fan's sake, with the books break, baseball
   can't take, a Gamblin' Rose.

While the case was being fought in the courts, Commissioner Giamatti remained silent. "My only frustration in all of this is that I can't hit a fastball, I can't hit
the cutoff man, I can only talk. And not being able to
talk is a test of my resolve, but I'm gonna do it."

Asked what he thought was the public's view of the
case, Giamatti said, "What I see is ongoing boredom. I
think most American fans are tired of this and I can
understand and share in that sentiment to some extent.
The game of baseball is independent of these pro-
ceedings."

During the long summer Rose made himself available
to reporters as if nothing were going on. And, to the surprise of many people, this was not the only subject he
spoke about. For example, he was sitting in the dugout
before a game one day when a writer asked him if he
thought he could hit .200 if he were still playing. "Hit
.200?" Rose said incredulously, "Shoot, Ray Charles
could hit .200. I mean, that's one for five. Ray has to be
able to get a hit a day, don't you think?"

Another day he told a reporter, "You know what I
don't understand? If a guy owns his own country, why
would he make himself a colonel? I mean, that guy
Khadafy in Libya, doesn't he run the place? Why is he
Colonel Khadafy? Why don't you think he made himself
a general?"

When several Reds players, including Eric Davis, complained that Riverfront Stadium's artificial surface was responsible for causing injuries, Rose responded, "I played on [turf] since 1965 and I never had an injury on it. Some guys are afraid to play on it. Some guys will get an injury looking at it. They'd get hurt going by a Monsanto factory."

Asked one day to name the best city to play in, he didn't hesitate. "If you had your wish, you'd go to San Diego and play every night—seventy-five degrees in the day, sixty degrees at night, no wind, no rain, and lots of girls in miniskirts."

But no matter where he went, or what he did, the specter of the case hung over him. When Reds infielder Ron Oester got into an argument with umpire Joe West, for example, Rose interceded. Later, when crew chief Jerry Crawford said that he had not even mentioned Rose in the official report he'd filed with the league office about the incident, Rose laughed and said, "That's about the only report I ain't been in this year."

When the Reds visited San Francisco in August, their hotel was jolted by an earthquake. Rose was in his room on the forty-first floor when the hotel started shaking. "Man, I got up and looked out my window and figured out that if the hotel had tipped over I would have come down five blocks away, in the middle of a Wendy's." Then he added, "Now they say there's a chance we might get another one in the next five days—and we're in town for three more days."

A reporter tried to reassure Rose, telling him that scientists were predicting that the odds against another earthquake hitting the same spot were 50 to 1.

Rose started laughing. "Don't talk odds to me," he pleaded. "Boy, are you talking to the wrong guy."

And after the Reds had traded outfielder Kal Daniels, who had been the subject of a lot of criticism in Cincinnati papers, to the Dodgers, Daniels complained, "I don't feel I got the publicity I deserved."

Rose laughed at that, too. "Believe me," he said, "publicity isn't what it's made out to be."

Finally, when the United States Court of Appeals denied Rose's petition to keep his action against Giamatti in an Ohio court, it became clear that the Commissioner intended to issue a decision whether Rose agreed to attend a hearing or not. Rose and his attorney met with the Commissioner and an agreement was reached. Commissioner Giamatti announced, in part, "Peter Edward Rose is hereby declared ineligible in accordance with Major League Rule 21 and placed on the Ineligible List.

"Nothing in this agreement shall deprive Peter Edward Rose of the rights under Major League Rule 15 (c) to apply for reinstatement...

"Nothing in this agreement shall be deemed either an admission or a denial by Peter Edward Rose of the allegation that he bet on any major league baseball game."

"I made some mistakes," Rose admitted in a statement issued after his suspension was announced, "and I think I'm being punished for those mistakes. However, the settlement is fair—especially the wording that says they have no finding that I bet on baseball... My life is baseball. I hope to get back into baseball as soon as I can... I've never looked forward to a birthday like I'm looking forward to my new daughter's birthday, 'cause two days after that is when I can apply for reinstatement."

Reaction to the decision was mixed. Henry Aaron said, "It's almost the same as giving him the electric chair."

Gary Carter wondered, "What are they going to do to him? Will they take away the road they named after him in Cincinnati, Pete Rose Way, too? Baseball is his life. Taking it away is like taking candy away from a kid."

Cincinnati councilman Steve Chabot assured everyone that there was only one way the name of Pete's road would be changed: "If the council's willing to call it Steve Chabot Way."

But Gold Star Chili announced that it had dropped Rose as its spokesperson, and the New York–Penn League left him off a poster honoring the stars who'd played in the league during its first fifty years in operation.

Many people wondered if the suspension would keep Rose out of the Hall of Fame when he becomes eligible in 1994. Jim Dwyer of the Expos said, as far as he was concerned, "The Hall of Fame is for baseball... Heaven is for good guys."

But in the truest test of American public sentiment, the day the suspension was announced the value of almost all items autographed by Rose went up. In fact, Rose appeared on the Cable Value Network that night selling autographed baseballs and other pieces of equipment. "I got the hits, I scored the runs, I made the plays," he said as he held up an autographed plaque selling for $79.92. "I don't think anybody can take that away from me."

A knowledgeable collector added, "He could go around the country as a one-man show [signing autographs] and make three times what he makes as manager of the Reds."

It's Still So, Joe

Before Rose, the best-known player banned from baseball for life was Shoeless Joe Jackson, a participant in the 1919 "Black Sox Scandal" in which members of the White Sox threw the World Series. Perhaps because of the Rose case, as well as the appearance of a Jackson character in the movies *Field of Dreams* and *Eight Men Out,* the South Carolina State Senate passed a resolution asking Commissioner Giamatti to restore Jackson as a "member in good standing of organized baseball."

The wonderful *New York Times* columnist Ira Berkow printed some recently discovered testimony from Jackson's trial. After admitting he'd accepted money from gamblers, Jackson was asked:

Q: Did you make any intentional errors yourself that day?
A: No sir, not during the whole series.
Q: Did you bat to win?
A: Yes.
Q: Did you run bases to win?
A: Yes, sir.
Q: And field the balls at the outfield to win?
A: I did... I tried to win all the games.
Q: Weren't you very much peeved that you only got $5,000 and you expected to get $20,000?
A: No, I was ashamed of myself.

Q: Where did you put the $5,000?

A: I put it in my pocket.

Q: What did Mrs. Jackson say about it?

A: She felt awful about it, cried about it awhile.

Q: Had you ever played crooked baseball before this?

A: No, sir, I never had.

Q: You think now Williams may have crossed you too?

A: Well, dealing with crooks, you know, you get crooked every way. This is my first experience and my last.

The Commissioner's office did not reinstate Jackson. But it seems to me that since he was banned for life, and he's no longer alive, he's no longer banned. If he could, he would be eligible to play. I wonder if the Senior League knows about this?

Sweet-Talking Griffey

Without question the Sweetest Story of 1989 is that of Ken Griffey, Jr. The nineteen-year-old son of Cincinnati's thirty-nine-year-old outfielder Ken Griffey surprised the Mariners in spring training when he unexpectedly played his way into the starting lineup. On Opening Day the Griffeys became the first father and son to be playing in the major leagues at the same time. When asked if being told he was going to open the season in center field for the Mariners was the greatest message he'd ever heard, Griffey Jr. said it was in the top three, along with "hearing your parents say they love you, and that you can buy the BMW."

Both Griffeys got off to slow starts. Griffey Jr. was 1 for 18. Griffey Sr., used mainly as a pinch-hitter, hit a home run, "otherwise, I would have been 0 for April." But both Griffeys finally started hitting. By the end of April, Junior's average was near .300 and he had been named the AL's Player of the Week.

After he'd broken a Mariners' record with eight consecutive hits, a Washington company decided to make him only the second major league player in history— Reggie Jackson was the first—to be honored by having a candy bar named after him. "He's as good as any player to come up in the last twenty years," the president of the candy company said. "He has the potential to be as good as any player in history." Then he revealed the real reason for marketing the candy bar this early in Griffey's career: "If we wait ten years [to do this], he would probably cost us a million dollars."

For the record, the Ken Griffey Jr. Milk Chocolate Bar contained 1½ ounces of milk chocolate and sold for 95 cents. It was made to look like a 2½″ × 3½″ chocolate baseball card, showing Griffey at bat and his signature molded into chocolate. The candy was covered in foil and the wrapper featured pictures of Griffey in action.

Only after the chocolate bar was on the stands was it revealed that Ken Griffey Jr. is allergic to chocolate. So he couldn't eat his own candy bar.

When the candy bar came out, a sportswriter suggested that they should have used mints instead of chocolate so that the candy could have been named Ken Griffey Junior Mints.

Meanwhile, Griffey kept improving as a player. After he'd made a brilliant throw to third base to nail the Tiger's Lou Whitaker trying to advance on a deep fly ball, Whitaker sent him a beer as a present. Griffey sent it back with a note pointing out, "I'm not yet twenty-one. I can't drink." And asked him to send a soft drink next time.

Griffey Sr. said he didn't hear from his son too often during the season. "He calls me more when he's not doing that well," he explained. "When he went 8 for 8 in that one stretch, I didn't hear from him at all." Griffey said his son's calls never last very long. "When it's his money he only stays on for five seconds."

There were inevitable comparisons made between the two Griffeys, but Doyle Alexander and Dave Stewart were the first pitchers to give up home runs to both of them. Ken Griffey Sr. wasn't interested in making comparisons, suggesting to writers, "Just say he looks like his mom and plays like his dad."

In a very close race, Griffey Jr. outhit Griffey Sr., .264 to .263. Maybe that's what's known as making your point.

The reverse of Ken Griffey Jr. was the Blue Jays' talented rookie Junior Felix. After watching Junior Felix hit a long home run, Oriole scout Ed Farmer said, "If he's Junior Felix, I'd really love to see Senior Felix."

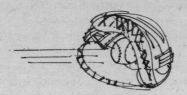

The I's Had It

Baseball is a game in which most players fail more often than they succeed. For example, a batter is a star if he hits safely three times in every ten at bats. A pitcher is a star if he wins more than half of his starts. So players get used to failing. That tends to make them honest about their mistakes. When pitcher Greg Cadaret heaved a pick-off attempt past Don Mattingly, allowing the runner to move to second, he explained, "I tried to put too good a pick-off move on him. And that's a problem because I don't have a good pick-off move."

Once, when Brad Kominsk was a young player coming up with the Braves, he was considered a potential superstar. But he never really made it. Now playing with the Indians, he admits, "I really don't consider myself a prospect. Maybe I'm a suspect now."

The Big Prospect of 1989 was Ben McDonald. The Orioles made him the number one draft pick in the country and, after prolonged negotiations, finally signed him for a contract worth almost a million dollars. Although McDonald is 6'7" tall, he told a television interviewer, "I don't see myself as 6'7", I see myself as just a normal 6'2" guy."

The Pirates' Andy Van Slyke had a very disappointing season, hitting only .237 with 9 home runs after signing a big contract. Toward the end of the year he explained, "I think I'm playing to erase some of the doubts from my mind, for the guys on this team and the management. I don't want to be a bad stock. I've split, but I don't want to plunge. My main goal is sanity."

Dodgers pitcher Ray Searage obviously understood exactly what Andy Van Slyke was talking about. "I've always got to be positive," Searage said. "I've got to think positive thoughts. If I don't, I become a nut-case."

Pitchers, of course, are the most self-critical players on the field. But they usually have the most reason to be. The Angels' Bert Blyleven, whose license plate reads: U B UGLY, admitted after pitching a bad game against the Red Sox, "I pitched like a meatball."

When Yankee Tommy John got taken out of a game in spring training he went for a long run. In the middle of that run, he stopped briefly to tell reporters, "I'm trying to burn off the frustration. I'll be right back, but first I'm going to try to kill myself."

And the Rangers' Charlie Hough, after losing to the Brewers for the ninth time without a win since 1982, explained, "It's not like it's one or two guys. It's if you're in a Brewers uniform, you're allowed to kill me."

My Kiner Guy

I was a broadcaster once. I lasted two seasons as a commentator at NBC. The main reason I lasted two seasons is because baseball went on strike my first season, saving my job for the second year. Look, the truth is that besides the fact that I mispronounced players' names, I got confused about statistics, I told stories that stretched for several innings then forgot the punch line, and sometimes I inaccurately described what was taking place on the field, I still did a terrible job.

I'm admitting this not because I want sympathy—it's a little late for that—but as a way of introducing this section on broadcasters. People make mistakes. NBC hired me, didn't they? And when a person is on the air live, hour after hour, day after day, eventually he is going to say something that other people find amusing. Except when I'm doing my comedy act, of course. I think a lot of broadcasters have a problem similar to that of Pedro Guerrero, who complained about newspaper reporters, "Sometimes they write what I say and not what I mean." There are quite a few broadcasters who really don't mean what *they* say.

The Mets' Ralph Kiner, for instance. Kiner is one of the most popular broadcasters in the business. His postgame show, *Kiner's Korner*, has been on the air in New York longer than any other program except *Meet the Press*. But sometimes, when the Hall of Fame slugger is doing play-by-play, he makes mistakes. In '89, for example, he did say that all of relief pitcher Steve Bedrosian's saves have come "during relief appearances." And he did say, "This is the first time the Mets have been at .500 since the third game of the year.

According to Kiner, the Pirates' Sid Bream was definitely in dangerous territory, because he "was playing a step behind the batter." Presumably he meant the runner.

One day Kiner gave Expos catcher Mike Fitzgerald credit for an interesting feat, saying he was 0 for 4 with 2 RBI and a base hit."

Noting that the father-and-son combination of Bobby and Barry Bonds was about to break the record for the most home runs by a father and son, Kiner said that the Bondses will "surpass the father-son tandem of Bobby Bell and Yogi Berra."

When Greg Jefferies hit a high pop-up in the infield, Kiner announced, "There's a foul pop-up into fair territory. [Bo] Diaz catches the ball in fair territory and Jefferies fouls out."

Trying to explain that the Expos had trouble stealing bases, he said, "They've been thrown out only one less time than the last-place team has been thrown out the most."

Ralph also told listeners, "Kevin McReynolds stops at third. He scores."

And perhaps the Malaprop of the Year Award goes to Ralph for his plea to Mets fans to "remember, it makes good sense to drink responsively."

And finally, on the final *Kiner's Korner* of the 1980s, Ralph introduced his guest, Tim McCarver, with his tongue tied firmly in his cheek, explaining, "Since this is the last *Kiner's Korner* of the decade, I got the most decadent guest I could think of."

Maybe just a little Kiner rubbed off on his broadcasting partner Rusty Staub, who complimented Kevin McReynolds by claiming, "There isn't a left fielder in the National League you could put on a par above him."

The Yankees' Phil Rizzuto has been behind a mike longer than Kiner. One of the most popular broadcasters in baseball, the Scooter makes no pretense of being neutral. The former Yankee shortstop is a Yankee fan. He roots openly for Yankees. Rizzuto has worked on both television and radio, but admits, "I like radio better than television, because if you make a mistake on radio, they don't know. You can make up anything on radio. On TV, they can tell." As an example of that, Rizzuto remembers the day he was working with his former broadcasting partner, now the American League president, Bill White. Rizzuto claimed a home run hit by Reggie Jackson had literally gone out of the ball park.

"Actually, Scooter," White said, "that ball landed in the seats."

"It doesn't matter," Rizzuto explained. "They can't see it anyway at home."

During one '89 game, Rizzuto's latest partner, George Grande, spoke about an event that was taking place in "bowels of the stadium." Scooter asked him to use another word, suggesting he say that it was taking place in "the inner sanctum of the stadium. See," Rizzuto explained, "imagine how that old-time radio show would have been if it had been called 'Tales from the Bowels.'"

Obviously New York does not have a monopoly on colorful broadcasters. The Cardinals' Mike Shannon, for example, told his listeners, after Orel Hershiser had walked a batter with the bases loaded, "Now that's a rarity you don't see very often."

And not all wonderful moments in broadcasting are mistakes. Every broadcaster has moments during the season when he finds just the right phrase to describe the situation of the field. After the Giants had signed the aging Goose Gossage, for example, who had been ineffective with the Cubs, Ralph Kiner quite accurately told his listeners, "The Goose is almost cooked."

After A's pitcher Curt Young sent the Angels' Glenn Hoffman sprawling in the dirt with an inside pitch, California broadcaster Joe Torre wondered, "Is that dustin' Hoffman?"

Early in the '89 season, Mets third baseman Howard Johnson was having a terrible time throwing accurately to first base. After one of his throws had skimmed the pitcher's mound and bounced once before reaching first, Tim McCarver wondered aloud if Johnson was simply trying to hit the cutoff man.

Bobby Murcer made a very good point after the A's Rick Honeycutt had picked off one Yankee runner, then had thrown over to first base several times attempting to keep Rickey Henderson close to the base, saying, "I know this sounds silly, but speed really slows down a game."

MSG cable's Greg Gumbel accurately described the White Sox' Ivan Calderon, who was wearing several chains around his neck, as wearing "a Mr. T starter kit."

Now: my choice of Comments of the Year: First runner-up goes to the Dodgers' Vin Scully, who said, describing the brief appearance on the mound by Dodger utility man Mickey Hatcher, "It's only the third time this year that the radar gun is smiling."

And the winner is...MSG cable's Tommy Hutton. During a Yankee-White Sox game, Chicago catcher Carlton Fisk was hit in the groin by a foul tip. As he rolled around in the dirt, in obvious pain, Hutton said softly, "I have two bits of advice for Fisk. Take a deep breath, and be glad he has a grown family."

The Radio Talk Show Call-in of the Year Call was made by Jackie McReynolds, wife of Mets outfielder Kevin McReynolds. After McReynolds had been criticized by members of the New York media for leaving the locker room so quickly after a game that he was gone before they got there to do their postgame stories, Jackie McReynolds called WFAN and explained that he left quickly to beat the traffic jams on the Long Island Expressway. The only problem with that, responded one writer, was that the game they were referring to was played in Chicago.

Another newspaperman wrote that he was pleased that

Jackie had finally made it clear to him why Mets outfielders insisted on playing so deep: "It's to be closer to their cars."

The biggest broadcasting story of the season was the purchase by CBS and ESPN of the rights to telecast major league baseball games, for which they paid almost $2 billion. That's "b" as in "boy, oh boy," not "m" as in "hmmmm." Nineteen ninety will be the first year in more than four decades that the Major League Baseball Game of the Week won't be seen on NBC, causing that network's excellent coordinating producer, John Filippelli, to dream, "Maybe CBS's check'll bounce and we'll get baseball back."

Ironically, it was at least partially the demands of prime-time television that forced the Chicago Cubs to finally install lights in Wrigley Field in 1988 and schedule eighteen night games in '89. So naturally, NBC Sports, exercising a clause in its contract with major league baseball, made the Cubs change the starting time of one of those eighteen games to 1:20 in the afternoon so the game could be broacast nationally.

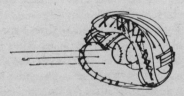

The Names of the Game

To some baseball fans, next to having talent, the most important thing a player can have is a great name, or nickname. According to *USA Today*, there have been 120 big league Smiths, 76 Joneses, 75 Johnsons, 58 Williamses, and 52 Wilsons, but it's the names that sound great, or the creative nicknames, that fans love to play with. ESPN announcer Chris Berman has become known for his ability to create great nicknames. His preseason 1989 All-Nickname lineup included: catcher Tony "Jala" Peña, first baseman Eddie "Eat, Drink, and Be" Murray, second baseman Steve "Alto" Sax, shortstop "Fettucini" Alfredo Griffin, third baseman Jim "Hound Dog" Presley, left fielder George "Taco" Bell, center fielder Oddibe "Young Again" McDowell, and right fielder John "I Am Not a" Kruk. Berman's starting pitchers were Bert "Be Home" Blyleven and Kevin "Totally" Gross, and his reliever was Jay "Thurston B." Howell. Since both his 1988 managers, Jim "Bela" Fregosi and Cookie "Days of Wine and" Rojas, had been fired, he hadn't named a new manager.

Berman's all-time ten Top Nicknames are: (1) John "Tonight Let It Be" Lowenstein, (2) Bert "Be Home" Blyleven, (3) Jim "Two Silhouettes on" Deshaies, (4) Julio "Won't You Let Me Take You on a Sea" Cruz, (5) Oddibe "Young Again" McDowell, (6) Von "Purple" Hayes, (7) Wally "Absorbine" Joyner, (8) Jose "Blame It on" Rijo, (9) Jim "Washer and" Dwyer, and (10) Jose "Can You See" Cruz.

The San Francisco Giants' popular broadcaster, Hank Greenwald, also a name game player, wondered on the air one night if Elmer Valo, the only Czechoslovakian-born big leaguer, was responsible for the Czech swing.

April 8 was a big day for the name-game players: listed among the pitchers losing games that day were Abbott and Costello—Jim Abbott of the Angels and John Costello of the Cardinals. I suspect those two players didn't think that was particularly amusing. And for older name-game players, April 6 was a memorable day as Montgomery beat Ward—the Royals' Jeff Montgomery out-pitched Toronto's Duane Ward. But the dream battery for the name game would have to be Twins pitcher Allan Anderson throwing to Indians catcher Andy Allanson. Obviously they would have to play for the A's.

Some people play the name game without even knowing it—Cardinal manager Whitey Herzog, for instance. When the Cubs' Mark Grace hit a wind-blown fly ball into the seats for his first career home run at Wrigley Field, Herzog called the blow a "disgrace."

San Francisco radio station KNBR ran a contest to find the best nickname for the Giants' slugging duo of Kevin Mitchell and Will Clark. The winning entry was the Pacific Sock Exchange. But certainly deserving of extremely honorable mention were such losing entries as Lumber Jocks, the Captains of Crunch, Clarksy and Clutch, Thriller and Killer, and—I don't know how they resisted this one—Great Pair of Knockers.

The 1989 award for the Best Nickname I'd Never Heard Before goes to White Sox first base coach Terry Bevington, who is affectionately know as " Psycho."

But without a doubt the Grand Wizard of Great Names is the Yankees' veteran public address announcer, Bob Sheppard. Sheppard, who also heads the speech department at New York's St. John's University, has made a study of euphonic names. That means names that sound good when he says them—believe me, when I say it, even "euphonic" doesn't sound good. Sheppards' All-Time Best Names to Pronounce over a Loudspeaker That Echoes list includes catcher Roy Campanella, first baseman Harmon Killebrew, second baseman Julio Franco, shortstop Jose Valdivielso, third baseman Mike Pagliarulo, left fielder Minnie Minoso, center fielder Joe DiMaggio, and right fielder (only on this team) Mickey Mantle. His pitchers are Salome Barojas, Cecilio Guante, and Luis Arroyo.

As a tribute to some of the sweetest-sounding ballplayers to appear in the big leagues, Sheppard wrote this "Poetic Tribute to Spanish Names":

> There are certain names that go over well
> Like Peña, Ramos, Carrasquel,
> With liquid sounds so panoramic,
> And strangely they are all Hispanic.
> Aurelio, Hipolito, Cecilio, Domingo
> Have a lovelier sound than American lingo
> What native name could I ever tell so
> Musically as Valdivielso?
> And no native name could ever show us
> The splendor of Salome Barojas.

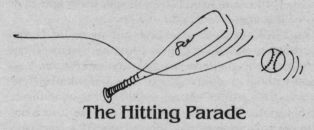

The Hitting Parade

The Mets' Greg Jefferies was pretty much a unanimous preseason choice to be the National League's Rookie of the Year. He got so much publicity after starring with the Mets in a late-season stint in '88 that to satisfy fans, he pointed out, "I would have had to hit 1.000, homer every time at bat, hit 200 home runs, and win a Gold Glove all in the same season." Instead, he opened the season in a prolonged slump, and many of his teammates openly resented his continued presence in the starting lineup. Only after he'd started hitting in midsummer did some of his teammates warm up to him. And that was when he learned one of the most important things a baseball player knows, as he said, "Hitting does bring friends."

Most players love to hit, or at least try to hit. For position players, that's what the game is all about. Offensively, the biggest surprise of 1989 had to be the NL's Most Valuable Player, Kevin Mitchell. After three mediocre seasons with the Mets, Padres, and Giants, Mitchell suddenly became one of the most dangerous hitters in baseball, finishing the season with a .291 average, a league-leading 47 home runs, and 125 RBIs. The reason for his emergence as a superstar, Mitchell explained, is that "I worked really hard in the off-season. I hit every day, day and night... I'm just trying to hit the ball where it's pitched. But the key is, you've got to swing the bat. Only the mailman walks."

One of the biggest surprises in the American League was Yankee shortstop Alvaro Espinosa. Given the job only after Rafael Santana had been injured and New York was unable to complete a trade, Espinosa, who had been unable to hit enough to play in the big leagues in several trials with the Twins, hit a solid .282. When asked how he'd suddenly become a good hitter, Espinosa explained that he had grown up in the Dominican Republic, a place where "you have to swing the bat, there are so many players that nobody can walk off the island."

The Padres' Tony Gwynn won his third consecutive NL batting championship, his fourth overall, with a .336 average. Opponents have so much respect for Gwynn that when a San Francisco reporter told Giants catcher Terry Kennedy that Ted Williams's vision was so good he could supposedly read the writing on the label of a rotating record, Kennedy replied, "That's nothing. I'll bet Tony Gwynn could read a CD."

Finishing three points behind Gwynn for the batting

title was the Giants' Will Clark, who added 23 homers and 111 RBIs. "This guy is not human," Kevin Mitchell said about Clark. "It's like somebody built him to play the game of baseball."

"When I get in my groove," Clark said when asked about his hitting ability, "the ball looks like it's got 'Hit me' written all over it."

Minnesota's Kirby Puckett led the major leagues in hitting with a .339 average. One of the reasons for Puckett's success, according to Twins teammate Al Newman, is that he's never satisfied. "The Puck's always saying, 'Newmy, I can't get any hits,'" Newman said. "He's hitting .330-something, I'm hitting .220, and I've got to listen to him complain about not getting hits."

During the '89 season the Yankees accused the Twins of using a camera in center field to steal their catchers' signals. Puckett laughed at the accusation, saying, "Stealing the signs? That wouldn't help me. I swing at everything anyway."

Puckett picked a bad time to go into his longest slump of the season. Needing only three hits in his next four games to break Joe Medwick's record for the most hits in his first five full big league seasons, Puckett went into an 0-for-15 slump. He ended up two hits short of tying the record. The first night of his sixth season, naturally, Puckett got two hits.

The AL's perennial batting leader, Wade Boggs, hit only .330 in '89. Boggs, the leading average hitter of the 1980s with a lofty .352 mark, is often criticized by the media for worrying more about his own performance than the team. In fact, a cartoon in *Boston Globe* this season showed Boggs at bat, looking at the catcher, and saying, "There are only three people who care if I get 200 hits. Me, myself, and Wade Boggs." Boggs finished with 205 hits, making everybody happy.

Among the hitters who reached personal milestones in '89 were Carlton Fisk and Ozzie Smith. Fisk got the 2,000th hit of his career in July. After going into a terrible slump as he got near the 2,000 mark, Fisk singled against the Yankees. When he reached first base the Chicago crowd gave him a huge ovation, causing Don Mattingly to ask him, "What's the big deal? You had another three months to get it."

Ozzie Smith, long honored for his fielding rather than his hitting, had the first five-hit game of his long career in '89. After the game, when a writer asked him if he had been aware that this was his first five-hit game, the Wizard of Ahs nodded and said, "Yeah. What do you want me to do, lie?"

There are some hitters that always seem to perform well in certain ball parks. Joe Carter, for example, always hit well in Fenway Park. Carter started the '89 season with a very ordinary .257 average in every park except Fenway, and in Fenway he was hitting .382, with 12 home runs. "This is the one park I look forward to coming to," Carter said, to the surprise of absolutely no one. "I live off the Wall [the short fence in left field]. You can miss the ball and still hit the Wall." Then Carter started talking about the huge billboard beyond the Wall that can be seen from home plate. "It advertises CITGO gas," he explained. "The first time I looked at the sign, that's what popped into my mind: See it go."

Baltimore's Billy Ripkin really hasn't hit well in the big leagues, but for the first few months of the season he was batting a solid .333 in night games. "I can see the ball better at night," he claimed. "Call me a vampire."

A lot of great hitters believe that one of the most important elements of success at bat is confidence. Some bad hitters, for example, are confident they're not going to get a hit. Others go to bat knowing they're going to get a hit. The Cardinals' Pedro Guerrero hit a strong .311, with 17 home runs and 117 RBIs, after a couple of subpar seasons with the Dodgers. Guerrero has always had confidence in his own ability, even when he wasn't hitting. After his two-run single with runners on second and third had beaten the Reds one night in '89, he told reporters candidly, "I would have walked me. I don't know what was on their mind."

Maybe the most personally satisfying hit of '89 belonged to Reds rookie Rolando Roomes. After playing nine seasons in the minor leagues, the twenty-seven-year-old outfielder got his chance to play in the major leagues when Eric Davis was hurt. He made his first start against the Mets at Shea Stadium. "My dream was always to play for the Mets," he said after getting a hit against them in the Reds' 6–4 win. "I was as diehard as fans get," Then he paused, shrugged and explained, "If you can't join them, beat them."

Hitting is tough; not hitting is easy. Anybody can't hit. Slumps are a big part of baseball, and absolutely every player goes into a slump from time to time. The difference between the good hitters and the bad hitters is the length of those slumps. Some slumps, for example, last an entire career. As Mets general manager Frank Cashen said about shortstop Kevin Elster, who hit well in the minor leagues but hasn't hit consistently in his two full big league seasons, "Until he hits, we won't know if he ever can."

Nobody has ever figured out why a player suddenly goes into a slump, but they have figured out the best way of getting out of one—get a few hits. "When you're in a slump," the Cubs' Vance law said, "it's almost as if you look out at the field and it's one big glove." "They shouldn't be called slumps," Astro infielder Bill Doran suggested while he was mired in a 9-

for-95 slump; "from now on they should be called Dorans."

The Pirates' Andy Van Slyke suffered through a season-long slump in '89. "I have an Alka-Seltzer bat," he explained. "You know—plop-plop, fizz-fizz. When pitchers see me walking up to the plate they say, 'Oh, what a relief it is.'" After going 0 for 6 in an extra-inning game, Van Slyke shook his head in frustration and said, "I've never been 0 for 6 before in my life." Then he corrected himself: "Well, maybe on the first six questions of a test." Among the many pitchers he claims he can't hit is Houston's Mike Scott. Van Slyke, who had one hit in 32 at bats in his career against Scott, said, "It's a good thing he wasn't born triplets, or I'd be pumping gas at Glenn Wilson's gas station."

When a player is in a slump, absolutely nothing goes right for him; players on the other team make spectacular defensive plays, every line drive goes right at somebody, he finally gets a few hits and the game gets rained out, and the frustration grows and grows. Lloyd Moseby struggled through a dismal .221 season in '89, with only 11 home runs and 43 RBIs. The highlight of the season for Moseby came in the final weekend series against Baltimore; he knocked in the winning run in the eleventh inning of the first game of the series with a long drive against the center-field wall, to clinch a tie for the division title for the Blue Jays. "If someone had caught that one," he said, summing up the frustration of the entire season, "I would have left the stadium right then, gone to my apartment, and hung myself."

During one stretch of the season Moseby was 0 for 22 and Tom Lawless, a career .207 hitter, was sent up to pinch-hit for him in the ninth inning of a one-run game against the Mariners. Lawless admitted he was very surprised to be used in that situation, explaining, "I'm usually the pinch-hittee, not the pinch-hitter."

Even players having good years, like Guerrero, go into slumps during the season. At one point during the season Guerrero was only 2 for 18 against left-handed pitchers. But at least he had a good reason for it. "I don't like them," he explained; "They throw with different hands."

Left-handed-hitting Yankee outfielder Mel Hall is another player who doesn't hit left-handed pitchers very well. During one stretch of the '89 season he spent almost two straight weeks on the bench while the Yankees faced a succession of left-handers. Finally, he got to start two consecutive games against right-handers. Asked after the first game if he was happy to be playing, he said, "When you're hungry, does it help to eat?"

A player will try almost anything to break out of a slump. Houston's Glenn Davis, for example, was hitting under .100 in day games played outdoors, until the day he decided to wear oversized amber sunglasses during the game. He hit the very first pitch thrown to him for a home run. "I took a lot of flak from the guys for those glasses," he said afterward. "They were saying, 'Hey Hollywood. Pretty Boy.'" Then he smiled and added, "But I got rave reviews from the umpires."

When California's Jack Howell was drowning in a deep slump, teammate Wally Joyner decided to help him out of it—he performed an exorcism on Howell's bat, setting it on fire. Howell hit a home run in the next game and reporters asked Joyner for details. "We're not allowed to talk about it [the exorcism]," he said solemnly. "It makes the baseball gods mad."

Houston's Gerald Young went to teammate Kevin Bass for suggestions on how to break out of his slump, and Bass told him to stop wearing batting gloves. Young tried that, and his average rose 35 points. Unfortunately, the skin on the palms of his hands became raw and painful. "That's okay," the happy Young said. "I'll just use a little spit, and a little pine tar."

There are times during a season when an entire team goes into a batting slump. When the Yankees stopped hitting, a reporter asked manager Dallas Green if he was worried about the fact that New York was going to be facing Cleveland's three tough starting pitchers, Rich Yett, Greg Swindell, and Tom Candiotti. Green said that it really didn't matter who was pitching against the Yankees, because "anyone who throws bothers our hitters."

And then there are teams that never go into a slump— they're not good enough. The '89 Dodgers, for example. When someone complimented Whitey Herzog on the success the Cardinal staff enjoyed against the Dodgers, Herzog shook his head and said, "You really can't judge your pitching against them, because those poor guys can't hit."

The Tigers were the worst-hitting team in the American League, but after they'd beaten the Blue Jays on two consecutive broken-bat hits in the ninth inning, Sparky Anderson said gratefully, "Those bats aren't healthy, but at least they died with honor."

The thing is, almost everybody—except major league players—believes he could hit if he had the opportunity. Once, before a Pirates game, four members of the Pittsburgh Penguins hockey team went out to Three Rivers Stadium and took batting practice against coach Rich Donnelly. After the workout, Donnelly summed up the hockey players' hitting skills. "They were all low-ball hitters," he said. "If you rolled it up there, they'd knock the hell out of it."

The most exciting hit in any game is the home run. It's the ultimate hit. And no player will ever forget his first major league home run. When the Cubs' Rick Wrona had hit his first big league homer, he was so happy he could barely control himself. After finally calming down, he explained his exuberance to reporters. "I couldn't help myself," he admitted. "You don't get your first homer too often."

The team with the least power in the major leagues in '89 was the Cardinals, who hit a grand total of 73 home runs. Maybe "grand" isn't exactly the right word. At one point during the season a sportswriter asked Herzog to predict how many home runs his club would hit. Herzog thought about it, then predicted confidently, "We'll catch Maris, sure as hell."

The Cleveland Indians had a powerful season one night, getting only six hits in a game against the Rangers—all of them home runs. The Indians never had a runner in scoring position during the game but still managed to score seven runs. "We were saying in the dugout," Joe Carter claimed, "that anyone who hit a single would be thrown out of the game and fined." The Indians got only three hits their next game, none of them singles—giving them seventeen straight innings without a single single.

Sluggers can have power shortages, just as other players go into batting slumps. For some unknown reason, they just stop hitting home runs. Two-time NL Most Valuable Player Dale Murphy had hit only 6 home runs through the first half of '89 when he suddenly exploded for the best single inning any batter had all season. Playing against the Giants, he had 2 home runs and 6 RBIs in one inning; in a week he hit a total of 5 homers. "Heck, it's great," Braves manager Russ Nixon said, then acknowledged the obvious: "He probably won't continue that hot…"

Giants manager Roger Craig saw things a little differently: "We woke him up, I'll say that…"

The Yankees' Don Mattingly has hit more than 30 home runs in three different seasons, but in '89 it took him almost two months and 159 at bats before he hit his first home run. "I was going to try to drive in 110 runs without hitting a homer," he told reporters with a straight face after the game. "Now I'm going to try to drive in 110 runs with only hitting one."

The Home Run of the Year was probably Bo Jackson's tremendous 448-foot clout on Rick Reuschel's second pitch of the All-Star Game. Before the game Reuschel had said about Jackson, "He's either going to swing and miss, or else he's going to hit one out."

But when Reuschel said that, I'm not sure he meant hit it out of the whole ball park.

The science of measuring the distance a baseball travels is not as exact as, say, underwater Tarot card reading, and there have been times when batters complain about the measurement. After Montreal's Tim Wallach had hit a blast officially measured at 396 feet, the Expos' oft-quoted PR director Richard Griffin decided, "Okay, let's call it 410 Canadian."

The Mets' Howard Johnson has become one of the NL's most feared sluggers in the past two seasons, and his newfound power has led several managers to check his bat to make sure it hadn't been corked. When Pete Rose heard that Montreal's Buck Rodgers had had Johnson's bat X-rayed, he suggested, "They ought to X-ray his arms."

In a lot of cases, the best thing about hitting a home run is that the player gets to trot leisurely around the bases—and in some cases that speeds up the game. For example, Houston catcher Alan Ashby hit his first triple in six years in '89, and had a tough time making it to third. "Like all great distance runners," he explained, "I hit the 'wall'... the difference is that I hit it as I rounded first."

That game took two hours and four minutes to play, causing Astros infielder Bill Doran to suggest, "If Ashby hadn't hit that triple, we might have been out of there in under two hours."

The near miss of the season on the bases was recorded by A's catcher Ron Hassey, who came within second base of running for a Piniella—that means running for the cycle, getting thrown out at every base in one game, as I saw Lou Piniella do. Against the Brewers one night, Hassey was thrown out at first, third, and home.

Catchers just can't run. That's obvious. After Giants catcher Terry Kennedy had stolen his first base of the season—of a lot of seasons, in fact—he proudly declared himself the first member of the Giants 1–1 club: he had one home run to go with his one stolen base.

Most first basemen can't run either. The Braves' forty-two-year-old Darrell Evans had his first triple in more than four seasons in '89. After the game a reporter asked him what he felt like chugging around the bases, and Evans told him "Aaaggggg, aaagggg..."

Red Sox first baseman Nick Esasky figured he'd finally come up with a way to increase his speed on the bases—he cut off his beard. "I'll be a little faster now," he said, explaining his theory, "because I've cut down on the wind drag."

And then there is the case of Pedro Guerrero, who has never been accused of being fast. Guerrero was very upset when Pirate pitcher Bob Walk, leading the game 5–0, refused to throw him a fastball. So when Guerrero hit a home run, he practically walked around the bases. His home run tour, clocked from the second he hit the ball until he touched the plate, took 37.2 seconds. Of course, that included the 13 seconds it took him just to get to first base.

I've seen Guerrero run, and I have just one question: Did people really know he was doing it on purpose?

There are some players who do know how to run, but very few of them can run like the Cardinals' Vince Coleman. Coleman set a major league record by stealing 50 straight bases without being thrown out, breaking Davey Lopes's old record of 38, before Montreal's Nelson Santovenia finally nailed him at second base. And then, the very next night, he got thrown out again.

And since I haven't quoted Richard Griffin in almost two full pages, I thought I'd mention that when Montreal's Kevin Dean and Otis Nixon both successfully stole bases during a spring training game, Griffin reported, "That's the first thing Nixon and Dean have stolen since Watergate."

And from the It Happens Every Season Department is the sad story of Blue Jays rookie Kevin Batiste. Batiste made his major league debut in the heat of the pennant race when Buck Rodgers put him in as a pinch-runner— and promptly got picked off first.

Strike of the Year

And from the It Never Happened Before in the Entire History of Baseball Department is the great story of pitcher Nolan Ryan. The real problem about writing about Ryan is that the numbers tend to overshadow the reality of his performance. In 1989, when Tommy John was released by the Yankees, Nolan Ryan became the oldest pitcher in baseball. And naturally Ryan began showing signs of slowing down.

On the highway, maybe. Certainly not on the pitcher's mound.

With his major-league-leading 301 strikeouts in '89, Nolan Ryan became the first pitcher in history to strike out more than 5,000 batters in his career. For the record, strikeout victim number 5,000 was Rickey Henderson, who said, "It was an honor for me to be part of it. When I came up to bat, I asked the umpire if I could take the ball out to him if I struck out and congratulate Nolan with it. But the catcher decided that he wanted to do it."

Then Henderson started talking about that particular at bat, telling reporters, "I was looking for a fastball."

No kidding, Rickey. It probably didn't take a whole lot to figure out that Ryan was going to throw him a fastball. Ryan is acknowledged to be the greatest fastball pitcher of all time. His fastball has been clocked by the radar gun at 100.8 mph—the fastest pitch ever recorded. The only other pitcher to throw more than 100 was Houston's J. R. Richard.

If there is a truly legendary figure in baseball, it's Ryan. The first time I ever worked behind the plate while he was on the mound, I ended up going to the eye doctor's office. I was hunched behind the catcher, Ryan's pitch came in—and just before it reached home plate, the ball exploded in about a million pieces. It was a terrible thing to see, or, in my case, to not see. The odd thing was, nobody else saw it. The catcher just caught the biggest piece, and threw it back to Ryan. Then, a few pitches later, it happened again. I had one thought: I wonder if it's too late to get back on the pro football disabled list?

I really thought there was something wrong with my eyes. Anyway, to make a short story long, the eye doctor explained to me that Ryan threw so fast that my eyes just didn't have time to adjust as the ball came closer. Ryan was actually faster than my eyes could see. After that I began calling his pitches by sound.

But everybody who has played the game with Ryan has that kind of story. Even when he was pitching in high school in Alvin, Texas, batters were afraid to bat against him. "At the start of the games I used to tell him to throw at batters," his high school coach, Jim Watson, admitted. "Heck, he was wild enough back then that I didn't need to tell him that, probably. By the second inning he could lob the ball up there and strike out people. They were too busy running out of the batter's box.

"I used to have a rule on my team that if anyone got hit by a pitch they weren't allowed to rub it because it looked like you were weak. I was taking batting practice against him one day and one of the first pitches he threw came right at my head. It was faster than anything I'd ever seen...It got me in the back. I could tell everybody was watching to see what I would do. I didn't rub it, but boy, was that a dumb rule."

Ryan remembered starting one game in high school by splitting the helmet of the first batter he faced, then hitting the second batter and breaking his arm. "The third guy," Ryan says, "begged not to hit."

Mets scout Red Murff's report on the seventeen-year-old Ryan might be one of the most accurate scouting reports ever filed. "Skinny, right-handed junior," Murff wrote. "Has the best arm I've ever seen in my life. Could be a real power pitcher someday."

"Someday" came two years later when he began his

big league career with the Mets, and big league hitters began learning what the high school kids in Alvin, Texas, already knew. "Guys don't know how lucky they are that Nolan found his control," former Dodgers infielder Davey Lopes says. "There was a time when he wasn't career-threatening, he was life-threatening."

"He is the only guy who ever put fear in me," Reggie Jackson said. "Not because he can get you out, but because he can kill you. There are no words to describe what it's like standing up there and seeing the ball coming at you. I simply couldn't do him justice. I like fastballs, but that's like saying I like ice cream—but not a truckload."

Ryan is one of the few major leaguers that other players are openly in awe of. "When I went up to bat against him," the Tigers' Dave Bergman said, "I was doing the best I could, but I was almost feeling, 'What am I doing on the same field with Nolan Ryan?'"

Len Matuszek went 7 for 12 against Ryan during his career—Ryan struck him out 7 of the 12 times he faced him. With Ryan, that's how you measure success. "I was a rookie and I went up to the plate batting .090. He just stared at me and gave me one of those get-in-there-and-stop-wasting-my-time looks. I hit a long one that had a chance to be a home run, but it curved foul. I was feeling pretty good about that until I looked at him. He was glaring at me. I knew I was in serious trouble."

Maybe even more amazing than the velocity of his fastball is the fact that he's still able to throw in the 90s after twenty-two big league seasons. In fact, after throwing that hard for that long, it's amazing he can even lift his arm to comb his hair. Hard throwers almost always burn out within a few years. But not Ryan. People judge events in their life by the length of his career. One day, for example, Montreal broadcaster Bobby Winkles, who had once managed Ryan with the Angels, recalled, "I realize now how long it is since I was fired as manager of the Angels. We had Nolan Ryan when he struck out his 1,000th batter."

When Ryan faced the Yankees for the first time in '89 after spending nine seasons in the National League with the Astros, several writers pointed out that he'd actually pitched against more Yankee broadcasters—Bobby Murcer, Lou Piniella, Tom Seaver, Jay Johnstone, and Tommy Hutton—than against active players. Ryan paid no attention to any of that, saying, "Writers like to say they've seen a lot of players come and go. Well, I've seen a lot of writers come and go."

If anything, Ryan is a better pitcher today than he was when he was younger. "Nolan wasn't the pitcher he is today when I caught his no-hitter in 1973," Jeff Torborg said. "He didn't have the change-up then. It was either fastball or curve. He was still pretty wild then. Against Boston one day he threw one a little up and over my shoulder. I reached for it—and the pitch tore a hole in the webbing of my glove and hit the backstop."

When he recorded the 5,000th strikeout of his career, sportswriters tried to find some way of putting it in perspective. They pointed out such things as, if a pitcher struck out 200 batters a year for 20 years, he'd still be 1,000 strikeouts short of Ryan. Then the Orioles' young pitcher Jeff Ballard was quoted as saying, "It would take me a hundred years to catch him." And *Baltimore Sun* writer Tim Kurkjian figured out that, in fact, if Ballard continued to strike out batters at his present pace, and averaged 30.5 starts a year, it would, indeed, take him precisely 100 years to record 5,000 strikeouts.

In compiling 5,000 strikeouts, Ryan struck out 1,066 different batters. The biggest contributor to that total is Claudell Washington, whom Ryan has struck out 36 times. Washington was very surprised when he heard that figure. "Is that all?" he asked. "I thought I had a lot more... All the at bats I've had against him have been bad."

"If he ain't struck you out," Davey Lopes once said, "you ain't nobody." In recording his 5,000 strikeouts, Ryan has struck out everybody from Henry Aaron to Paul Zuvella. He's struck out 17 Hall of Famers and 42 players who have won Most Valuable Player awards. He's struck out 7 of the 16 players who compiled 3,000 hits, 7 of the 14 sluggers who hit more than 500 home runs, 27 batting champions, and 33 home run champions. He's struck out 13 different Davises, the most of any name; he's struck out presidential names Jefferson, Carter, Wilson, Ford, and Bush; he's gotten the colors Green, Blue, White, and Brown, as well as "Le Grand Orange," Rusty Staub. He's gone about the task very religiously, striking out Jesus Alou, a Moses, and several Matthews, Marks, and Johns. He's taken care of baseball's royalty, striking out a King, Queen, Knight, and Duke. He's gone into the wilderness to strike out a Moose, a Bird, a Deer, and a Bass. He's struck out three players who were born after he struck out pitcher Pat Jarvis in September 1966, for his first big league strikeout, he's struck out six current major league managers, two general managers, a player in the National Basketball Association, and a player in the National Football League. Keeping it in the family, he's gotten 10 different sets of brothers and 6 sets of fathers and sons—the Bonds, Willses, Griffeys, Franconas, Alomars, and Schofields. And he's struck out both a Law and a Lawless.

It isn't just the strikeouts that guarantee him a featured spot in the Hall of Fame. Ryan has also pitched 5 no-hitters, more than any pitcher in history, and 10 one-hitters.

Five different times he's gone into the ninth inning needing three outs for another no-hitter—and given up at least one hit. For the record, the ten players who cost Ryan a no-hitter are Denny Doyle, Carl Yastrzemski, Thurman Munson, Alex Johnson, Bob Stinson, Duane Kuiper, Reggie Jackson, Terry Kennedy, Tim Flannery, and Nelson Liriano.

Among the 38 major league records Ryan holds is most walks. Ryan's strikeouts don't seem to ensure victories for his team—in fact, the complaint heard most often about Ryan is that his ratio of wins to losses is not particularly impressive. Well, it is to me, but not to some baseball people. For example, one night in '89 he struck out 14 Blue Jays in 6 innings—but still lost the game, 4–0. As Toronto's Mike Flanagan said after that ball game, "It looks like our problem this year has not been striking out enough." Flanagan, incidentally, claimed that one of the main reasons Ryan throws so fast is that he grunts every time he releases a fastball. "I used to throw much harder myself," he claims, "but I tore my vocal cords when I was a kid and haven't thrown as hard since."

The team that has given Ryan the most difficulty during his career has been the Baltimore Orioles. Since Ryan no-hit them in 1975, he's only 1–11 against them in 15 starts. The last time he beat them was in 1976, or at least a full career ago for a normal player.

There's really never been a pitcher like Ryan. Several times in '89 the Giants aging pitcher Rick Reuschel was compared to him. Reuschel laughed at that. "Anybody who talks about me and Nolan Ryan in the same vein has mush for brains. The only possible comparison is that we're both in our forties."

"If there is such a thing as the eighth wonder of

the world," Seattle manager Jim Lefebvre said, "it's him."

Tommy Lasorda agrees, suggesting, "When he's through, they'd better send his arm to the Smithsonian."

That, of course, is the big question: How long can he continue to pitch? Asked about that, Ryan says knowingly, "When I lose my fastball, I'm gone."

So now we know the answer to that question. Never.

Baseball's Relatives

Baseball is a very big business, particularly in the world of entertainment. In books, movies, on television, in music, baseball was a very popular subject in '89. The best-seller among the dozens of baseball books published was David Halberstam's *Summer of '49*, the story of the 1949 baseball season, focusing on the American League pennant race between the Red Sox and the Yankees.

Other popular baseball books included *Total Baseball*, a huge 2,294-page reference book advertised by its publisher as "The Most Complete Baseball Encyclopedia Ever." Unfortunately, due to a printing error, 17 players whose names began with the letter Z were left out of the book, causing coeditor John Thorn to complain, "Someone at the printing plant was catching some zzzzz's."

Probably the most controversial book of the year was Toronto catcher Ernie Whitt's autobiography, *Catch*, in which he claimed that umpires hold grudges against certain teams and, in particular, "Joe Brinkman hates our ballclub... Every close call with Brinkman and his crew goes against the Jays." I got a little upset when I read that remark. First, because Joe Brinkman is an excellent umpire who has always called them precisely as he sees them, without any regard for the uniform; and second, because of the inference that umpires cheat. The fact is that by the time an umpire reaches the major leagues he no longer thinks on the field—he reacts. By that I mean that an umpire has made so many calls in his minor league career that he does everything instinctively—he seesaplayandcallsit in a split second. He doesn't have time to think, "Hmm, it's close, but Whitt's playing for the Blue Jays and I don't like that team, so I'm going to call him out."

It's almost impossible for an umpire to be biased against a team, and it's a good thing I'm no longer an active umpire or I'd make Whitt pay for that remark.

Yogi Berra's autobiography, *Yogi: It Ain't Over*, written with Tom Horton, was published in '89. When a reporter asked Yogi what the book was about, he supposedly replied, "I don't know. I haven't read it yet." Supposedly.

Orel Hershiser collaborated with Jerry Jenkins on his autobiography, *Out of the Blue*. George V. Higgins's *The Progress of the Seasons* is the story of the Red Sox since the mid-1940s, as seen by someone who started his love affair with baseball as a short-suffering Red Sox fan, served his suffering apprenticeship, and can now proudly call himself, a long-suffering Red Sox fan. Of course, that makes me wonder: Is a short Red Sox fan a short long-suffering Red Sox fan? The great broadcaster Harry Caray wrote his autobiography, *Holy Cow!*, with the help of Bob Verdi. Robert Whiting's *You Gotta Have Wa* was about Japanese baseball, and *El Beisbol* by John Krich, was about baseball in the Caribbean. Frank Deford finally revealed the real truth about the so-called Mighty Casey in his novel *Casey on the Loose*, which told the story of what really happened after Casey went to bat and struck out. Ira Berkow combined notes Hank Greenberg had dictated before his death with his own research to write *Hank Greenberg: The Story of My Life*. And the revised edition of Paul Dickson's *Baseball Dictionary* was published. Among the additions was the phrase "Game six." Apparently that phrase is used in the Boston area to describe anything terrible, a reference to the disastrous game six of the 1986 World Series between the Red Sox and Mets.

And, naturally, the softcover edition of my fourth book, the warm, witty, wonderfully amusing look at baseball history entitled *Remembrances of Swings Past*, written by me, Ron Luciano with David Fisher, was published by Bantam. Not to disparage any other books, but believe me, my book is great. To quote me, as I wrote in my book, *Remembrances of Swings Past*, published by Bantam, "I will never make the Hall of Fame, I'm not in any record books, umpires aren't even listed in *The Official Encyclopedia of Baseball*, and I never appeared on a baseball card, but it makes me feel good to know that whenever people remember my career, they're going to laugh...

"Characters are born and made. Doug Rader, a Certified Character of the Game, who once claimed that his bats had been quarantined because of Dutch Elm Disease, believed, "Being a character is something you work up to. You have to serve a culprithood." That quote is from my book, *Remembrances of Swings Past*, published by Bantam.

Baseball was also a popular subject in the movies in 1989. Among the pictures shown in theaters or released on video were *Major League, Field of Dreams, Eight Men*

Out, and *Bull Durham*. Other films that had baseball scenes in them included *The Naked Gun*, *The Dream Team*, *Stealing Home*, and *Night Games*.

Major League, the story of the mythical Cleveland Indians (as opposed to the real Cleveland Indians), introduced characters like the relief pitcher known as the "Wild Thing" and a slugger who depended on voodoo for his success. In the film the team comes together to fight an owner who wants them to fail so the Indians can be moved out of Cleveland. It's easy to tell this movie is a fantasy because in it the Indians overcome a complete lack of talent to win the pennant, something the real Indians have not been able to do since 1954. The real Indians gave this film mixed reviews. "I was really juiced at the end," Tom Candiotti said. Catcher Joel Skinner saw it differently, explaining, "Basically, it's the story of union against management. Employees rallying together for the benefit of the organization. They used baseball, but it's like any other business."

Yeah, sure, Joel, like any other business in which you get paid three or four hundred thousand dollars for hitting .230.

The most popular baseball film of 1989 was *Field of Dreams*, starring Kevin Costner. In it, a farmer is in his field one day when he hears a voice telling him, "If you build it, he will come," and realizes that that means he's supposed to rip out his cornfield and build a baseball field so the dead Shoeless Joe Jackson can come out of the cornfield at night to play baseball. Somehow, it all works, the field and the movie. A lot of people were crying at the end, and that had nothing to do with the fact that they had paid $7.50 for a ticket. The film is really about fathers and sons and faith and fantasy. Comedian Billy Crystal did a special for cable television in which his voice tells him to go to Russia, saying, "If you go, take a coat."

The farmer on whose land the baseball field was built for the movie has kept the infield intact, but, he says, "With all the media coverage, people are really starting to bother us. It's sort of getting out of hand. I guess I'm keeping the dream alive." Then he added, "But I don't hear voices yet."

Brief clips of major league players in action were used in several other films. Pitcher Al Leiter appeared in *The Dream Team*, the story of a group of men from an insane asylum trying to get to Yankee Stadium. Somehow, I think that's appropriate. They get separated on their way to the Bronx and one of them becomes manager of the Yankees. Okay, part of that last sentence isn't true, but I leave it to each reader to figure out which part that is.

A short clip of Tom Brookens catching a foul ball is used in the comedy *The Naked Gun*. "I'll tell you one thing," Brookens said, "I never got paid for it... But the thing that bothers me is that I definitely didn't get top billing."

Practically every big league team released a video highlight film in '89. Even the Seattle Mariners sold a fifty-nine-minute video entitled *The Seattle Mariners: A Diamond in the Emerald City*. Now, I love the city of Seattle. The people I know from Seattle are very nice and very warm. The restaurants there are very good. There's a reason that Seattle is rated high among the best places to live in the entire United States. But I do have one question: Where did they get fifty-nine minutes of highlights?

I've seen that team play, so I could understand, say, twenty minutes—with just a little stretch. But an hour? Seattle has never been a great baseball team; what could they possibly put in that video? The thing I remember most when I think of Seattle baseball is that the popular Tom Paciorek once made a personal appearance in a supermarket and they put him in the frozen food section—and then asked him to move because he was hurting the sales of frozen foods.

I'll bet you that's not on the tape. If it were, that tape would have been a full hour.

Mickey Mantle appeared in two videos released in '89. In *Mickey Mantle: The American Dream Comes to Life*, the Mick tells about the day he was flying to Dallas and thought he was having a heart attack on the airplane. "I made up a story for the press," he says in the video. "I told them that that night I dreamed that I had died and gone to heaven. I got in to see God. But God said, 'Sorry, Mickey, we can't keep you here because of the way you acted on Earth. But,' he said, 'before you go back, would you sign these two dozen baseballs for me?'"

The second video he starred in, *Play Ball with Mickey Mantle*, has caused him some problems. This is an instructional tape, and most of the exercises demonstrated on the tape are supposed to be done outdoors. But there is a simple base-stealing exercise that's supposed to be done inside. The viewer is supposed to lay down a piece of paper on the floor to be used as first base, then take a short lead off that base while, on the tape, Tom Seaver goes into the stretch position. The object is to figure out when Seaver is going to throw over to first base and get back to the base before he does.

After trying to do that, one viewer sued. I guess Seaver's pick-off move was better than he figured. "He had sneakers on," his negligence attorney explained, "not cleats, and when his foot hit the piece of paper, it obviously slid, propelling him across the room and into a wooden desk." The results included a fractured ankle, severed tendon, and torn ligaments.

That's some tape—it even comes with real Mickey Mantle injuries. See it once and your legs are in as bad shape as his were. There is no word, incidentally, of the disposition of the lawsuit.

Orel Hershiser appeared in a video clip, too, although in his case it was unexpected. "I went to about three [National Basketball Association] Los Angeles Clippers games," he said, "but they must be saving the videotape because I've seen myself showing up on the TV news highlights supposedly attending about seven games." When asked why he preferred the Clippers to the more popular Lakers, he said, "You can't get good tickets to the Lakers games. At the Clippers games, you can sit on the floor, on the bench... They'll even let you play if you want..."

Several baseball players made musical appearances during the '89 season. Pinch-hitter Thad Bosley is a noted pianist who has released an album; amateur drummer Steve Sax sat in with the Beach Boys when they performed at Yankee Stadium after a ball game; Cubs outfielder Dwight Smith sang the national anthem before a game, becoming the first player to perform the anthem at Wrigley Field since third baseman—trumpeter Carmen Fanzone did it in 1972; and Padres infielder Tim Flannery joined singer Jimmy Buffett in a duet of Buffett's megahit, "Margaritaville." "I've played in the playoffs, I've played in the World Series, and I've sung with Jimmy Buffett," Flannery said after his performance. "What else is there?"

Flannery wasn't the only singing Padre. Pitchers Greg Booker and Mark Grant wrote and recorded a rap song extolling their teammate Bruce Hurst, who doesn't drink alcohol or anything with caffeine in it:

> His very first outing was the worst of all year,
> When he came into the clubhouse he almost had a
> beer.

After a game, he's thirsty as can be,
He reaches for a Coke, caffeine-free."

A Minor Report

To the players, there is nothing minor about the minor leagues. Every at bat, every pitch they throw, can be a step toward the big leagues. Only after they get to the big leagues do the things they did in the minor leagues seem minor. It seems to me that the Minor Feat of the Year has to be the performance of Vancouver Canadians pitcher Tom Drees, who pitched three no-hitters in 1989, two of them in a row. For the record, the last time a pitcher in professional baseball threw three no-hitters in one season was in 1952, when Bill Bell did it while pitching for Bluefield in the Appalachian League.

Drees, a White Sox farmhand, had shoulder surgery in the winter of '88 and opened the '89 season with only two wins in five decisions. But then, on May 23, he threw a nine-inning no-hitter against the Calgary Cannons, beating them 1–0. Five days later he threw his second no-hitter, this one in a seven-inning game against the Edmonton Trappers. In the Minor Understatement of the Year, Drees said, "I never would have expected it."

There was great anticipation before his next scheduled start, as Drees attempted to become the first pitcher in the history of professional baseball to pitch three straight no-hitters. "If he gives up a hit," Vancouver pitching coach Moe Drabowsky said, "we'll have to pull him out of the game."

Drees managed to no-hit Albuquerque for...less than an inning. The Dukes' Tracy Woodson homered off him in the first inning. "It was kind of a relief to see it end," Drees admitted, "but I could think of better ways than a homer."

It took Drees another three months before he finally pitched another no-hitter, beating Las Vegas. "I've been struggling of late," he said—of course, after what he'd done, giving up two hits could be considered struggling. "To be honest, I was tiring a little in the last two innings, but obviously I'm thrilled the way things turned out." And what was Drees's reward for his incredible season? At the end of the year the White Sox sold his contract to Vancouver.

Another pitcher who had a no-hitter going for just a little while was Willie Smith of Salem in the Class A Carolina League. In 3⅔ innings against Winston-Salem, Smith didn't give up a hit—just nine walks and five earned runs. Smith is the same pitcher who gained recognition by replying, when asked how big his high school was, "Five stories."

I guess the minor leagues can best be described as the place where you often see things that you'll never see again. Describing Drees's two consecutive no-hitters, Vancouver manager Marv Foley said, "You'll probably never see that again as long as you live."

Twins minor league clubhouse man David McQueen expressed a similar sentiment, saying, "We'll probably go the rest of our lives and never see another like it." The difference, though, is that McQueen was talking about the Minor Hit of the Year, not a no-hitter. The hit was a ground-rule double in the Appalachian League by the Martinsville Phillies slugger Tommy Hardgrove. Sixteen years ago a Martinsville carpet store owner hung a basketball hoop on the center-field fence 440 feet away from home plate, and offered $1,000 to any player who could hit a ball into the net. Sixteen years went by. An estimated 150,000 batters came to the plate in the ball park and took a shot at it before Hargrove accomplished the feat and won the $1,000. "It got to the point it took so long that we thought it was never going to happen," the carpet store owner said. "Last winter we talked about raising it to $10,000, just to add a little excitement. Procrastination is a blessing sometimes."

Why do I think he was smiling when he said that?

Everything in the minor leagues tends to be unpredictable, from the quality of play to the weather. For example, the Rangers' Class A Butte, Montana, team was snowed out of its second home game of the season. That's not too unusual, according to co-owner John McCurdy, who reminded everybody, "Let's put this in perspective. Summer doesn't begin officially for three days."

Then there was the odd record set by the Charleston, West Virginia, Wheelers—who had nine straight home games rained out. Fittingly, their opponent for the ninth game was supposed to be the Charleston, South Carolina, Rainbows. Now, the truth is that I really don't know if having nine straight games rained out was a Charleston Wheelers record. But I really hope so.

Of course, what the Triple A Phoenix Firebirds should have done was move to Charleston. Instead, to combat the blazing summer heat in Arizona, the Firebirds installed baseball's first Cool Mist section. Three hundred nozzles were attached to the stadium roof, and when the system was turned on they emitted a mist that supposedly cooled the air in the section between fifteen and twenty degrees. The system's designer claimed that it served the same function as "300 tons of air conditioning." Or one West Virginia rainstorm.

Certainly the Very Minor Deal of the Year was made by the Class A Reno Silver Sox, who sold pitcher Tom Fortugno to Stockton. Originally, Reno wanted $5,000 for Fortugno, but after some very tough negotiations they settled for $2,500—and 144 baseballs.

Outfielder Mark Davidson pulled the Minor Miracle of the Year, actually being in two places at once at different times. In a Pacific Coast League game, Davidson started in right field for the Twins' Portland team in a game against Tucson, but the game was suspended because of rain. Before it could be rescheduled, the Twins traded Davidson to Houston, who assigned him to Tucson. When the game was finally resumed, Davidson was in left field for Tucson, thereby appearing in the box score as a player for both teams.

My personal choice for Bird Brainstorm of the Year was accomplished by Mal Finchman, manager of Boise in the Class A Northwest League. After an umpire had ejected Finchman from the game, the manager returned to the field disguised as the team's mascot, Humphrey the Hawk. Why the man was a hawk and not a finch, I have no idea. "I did it so I could still have contact with my players," he chirped after the game. As it turned out, maybe he should have just flown the coop, so to speak, as Boise lost, 8–4.

Actually, Finchman wasn't the first manager to don a disguise. Several years ago Ed Nottle did the same thing during a Pacific Coast League game, but Nottle got caught by the umpire because he was the only person on the field wearing a tiger costume and baseball shoes.

Nottle, coincidently, managed the Red Sox' Triple A Pawtucket team in '89. After his team had blasted the

Scranton–Wilkes Barre Red Barons, 26–3, he said, in the Minor Understatement of the Year, "If we swing the bats like that, we're going to win a lot of games this season."

On the subject of birds, the great Rocky Bridges spent the summer of '89 managing Salem in the Class A Carolina league. During the season, Bridges, who was rarely seen during his career without a big chaw of tobacco lodged firmly in his cheek, got upset because his players preferred to chew sunflower seeds. "Sunflower seeds," he said, shaking his head disgustedly, "that's for birds to eat. I'm just afraid my players will start molting or going to the bathroom on newspapers."

Umpires start in the minor leagues just as players and managers do—and most umpires finish in the minor leagues, just as players and managers do. Working in the minor leagues gives young umpires experience in making the kind of tough decisions that prepare them for the big leagues: for example, are eight players too many to throw out of one game? My choice for the Minor Ejection of the Year took place during a Texas League game between Midland and Wichita. After umpire Brian Owen ruled that Midland's catcher had trapped a ball against the screen behind home plate, rather than caught it cleanly for the out, the Midland P.A. announcer decided to broadcast a few bars of the Linda Rondstadt song "When Will I Be Loved?" Unfortunately, the few bars he chose began with the statement "I've been cheated, been mistreated..." That was all Owen had to hear—he ejected the P.A. announcer. Next to go was Midland's manager, who argued about the call. Later in the game a fight erupted, causing Owen to get another six players. So the young umpire had a good afternoon: six players, one manager, and one P.A. announcer. I've got to like this kid. I've never met him, but he reminds me of my friend Kenny Kaiser when Kenny was younger. When he was in the minor leagues, he didn't just stop at the P.A. announcer—he once ejected the entire press box. Cleared them all out. I suspect that Kenny would have handled the situation in Midland just as Owen did, but knowing Kenny, he probably would have gone just a little further—he would have tracked down Linda Rondstadt and ejected her, too.

For the record, when the Arizona State League hired Theresa Cox in 1989, the number of female umpires working in professional baseball immediately doubled—to two. Pam Postema, who'd been in baseball thirteen years, spent her seventh season in Triple A. For the new record, the firing of Pam Postema at the end of the '89 season cut in half the number of female umpires working in professional baseball. Postema was released because it had become apparent she was never going to make it to the big leagues.

Cox believes that "being a good umpire is a God-given talent. You're abused even when you get the call right, which is 99 percent of the time. So you have to have an inner toughness. I'm a person you can count on to run a game and not be temperamental. I have my principles, though. In my first game, I walked twenty-two batters until they finally found my strike zone."

In that respect, Cox is right. Because when God gave me the talent, He not only gave me the inner toughness, He was nice enough to give me a big outer shell. In fact, He gave me a strike zone so big that pitchers can find it with a map.

There always seems to be something different happening in the minor leagues, and '89 was no different. For example, the Quad City Angels of the Class A Midwest League lost their shirts after one game—literally. South Bend, Indiana, police seized Quad City's uniforms, bats, and helmets because of a disputed hotel bill. The police then guarded all the exits from the clubhouse and searched each player as he left the locker room, undoubtedly to make sure the players weren't trying to smuggle out bats under their shirts. Quad City Angels general manager Mike Tatoian complained that the police had no legal right to seize the equipment because it was the property of the California Angels, not Quad City. "If they felt they had to seize something, they can come here and get a popcorn cart."

The Biggest Minor Strike was the one called by the Vancouver Canadians, who forfeited a game to Albuquerque, 9–0, because they hadn't received their bimonthly salary checks. The team was paid after the game. The Canadians' general manager Brent Imlach, briefly considered suspending or fining several of the players. That would have been something to see—taking money away from players who were protesting because they hadn't been paid in the first place.

As far as I'm concerned, the Minor Event of the Year took place in Tacoma, Washington. When a Tacoma player hit a grand slam home run, several spectators just happened to notice a man standing on the roof of a school a little beyond the outfield fence, dressed completely in black and *firing an automatic weapon*. Well, I guess you can imagine how that interfered with the baseball game. The umpires immediately called time, because of a man dressed in black firing an automatic weapon. Obviously it was the right thing to do, since nobody objected. There is no ground rule covering people dressed in black firing automatic weapons. "I didn't know what was going on," said Tucson's third baseman, Chuck Jackson, who took one look and dived for cover. Jackson continued, maybe just a little unnecessarily "Anytime I see guns like that, I get nervous."

While Tacoma's radio announcer was calmly asking his listeners to call 911 immediately and get the police, Tacoma's general manager got in his car and drove toward the school to see what was going on. As he approached the school he saw several more figures dressed in black. He turned the car around and headed back to the stadium, ready to order an evacuation.

Boy, there are some times when I really miss the fun in the minor leagues.

It was not so quickly discovered that the Tacoma Police Department Special Weapons Tactics Squad was conducting a training exercise—with dummy ammunition.

The primary purpose of the minor league system is to provide players for the major leagues. The 1989 winner of the Perseverance Award is Matt Winters, who spent 11⅓ seasons, 1,259 games, and 4,948 at bats in the minor leagues before finally becoming, at age twenty-nine, the oldest rookie of '89. There were times, Winters admits, when he considered quitting. After the '86 season, for example, he took a job in a frozen food factory, but quickly discovered "working in a frozen food factory isn't the same as playing baseball."

He finally made his big league debut when Kansas City called him up at the end of May, and in his first big league at bat—he doubled. That really shouldn't be a surprise. I mean, the guy had been practicing for that at bat for 11⅓ years. In 107 at bats with the Royals, Winters hit .234, with 2 home runs.

Another player who made his big league debut in '89 was Tiger rookie Jeff Datz. His welcome to the big leagues was a fastball that hit him, thrown by the Royals' Jeff Montgomery. "I went up there looking for something to hit," Datz said, "I guess he was, too."

Of course, what goes up must come down—at least sometimes. After Cincinnati's rookie pitcher Scott Scudder had been hit hard several times, the Reds decided to send him back to the minor leagues. The Reds were in Los Angeles when general manager Murray Cook asked Scudder to come to his room. As Cook was telling Scudder that he had decided to send him back to Nashville, an earthquake hit. The two men stared at each other until the quake subsided, then Scudder asked, maybe a little nervously, "Does the room always shake when you tell players they're going down?"

Several other former big leaguers, besides Pete Falcone, appeared in minor league lineups in the summer of '89. The great relief pitcher Tug McGraw signed a one-day contract to pitch for former NFL star Roman Gabriel's Gastonia Phillies in the Class A South Atlantic League. McGraw pitched five innings, giving up only one run. But attendance at the ball park, which had been averaging slightly less than 700 a game, was a hefty 4,168. I know you've been wondering, if nineteen-year-old Ken Griffey, Jr., was the youngest player in the major leagues in 1989, who was the oldest player in the minor leagues? The answer to that question is fifty-year-old Pete Richert. Richert, pitching coach for Modesto in the California League, pitched a perfect 1–2–3 inning when his club ran out of pitchers while being routed by Stockton, 11–1. Richert set a new California League record for the longest rest between appearances, having last pitched in the league just thirty years ago. That easily shattered the old record of twenty-three years, set by Don Sutton in '88, when he pitched in the league during a rehabilitation stint. And that's the minor fact of the year.

Finally, the Minor League Names of the Year are Kevin Brown and Buenaventura Rodriguez. According to the Brewers' 1989 media guide, Kevin Brown pitched an incredible 427 innings in the minor leagues in 1988. That comes to slightly less than four innings a game—every game of the season. Obviously, that would put a real strain on any pitcher's arm. And the fact is that the Brewers mistakenly added up the total innings pitched by all the Kevin Browns in the minors: Kevin A. Brown of the Brewers, James Kevin Brown of the Rangers, and Kevin D. Brown of the Mets. So, if this should ever turn up on *Believe It or Not*, the correct answer is: Not.

Buenaventura Rodriguez played with Montreal's Class A farm team in Jamestown, New York, in 1989. In fact, he didn't have a particularly good season, but Montreal PR director Richard Griffin, who hasn't been mentioned in several pages, loved Rodriguez's name so much that he included an update in the notes he issued to reporters before each game. Admittedly, sometimes Griffin had to stretch to find something to write about his prize prospect. For example, before one game he announced, "Jamestown was off yesterday. Buenaventura Rodriguez did his laundry."

Public Defenders

Maybe the thing I loved watching most when I was on the field was a great defensive play. Once Amos Otis made an incredible over-the-shoulder catch in center field that was so good that I ran right out there next to him and started applauding.

And then there were the fielders who weren't so good. Players like first baseman Dick Stuart. One day I was watching a boxing match with my old partner Bill Haller, and at the end of the fight the loser, who had really been beaten up, claimed, "He didn't lay a glove on me." Haller looked over at me and said, "You know, that's exactly the same thing baseballs say about Dick Stuart."

So, in the category of defensive play, the 1989 Catch of the Year Award goes to...Wade Boggs's wife, who caught Wade and Margo... No, no, that's not true. The Catch of the Year Award goes to the Giants' left fielder Kevin Mitchell. A lot of players in the history of baseball have made one-handed catches—but almost all of them used the hand with the glove on it. Not Mitchell. Playing against the Cardinals, Mitchell ran a long way into foul territory trying to catch up to a drive hit by Ozzie Smith. Mitchell actually overran the ball, so he had to reach up over his shoulder with his bare hand to catch it. That catch was so good it's even exciting just to imagine it. An amazed Terry Kennedy said after the game, "After he caught it, he should have just ripped the cover off the ball with his teeth and thrown it to the crowd."

Outfielder Brady Anderson was so impressed that he decided, "That would have even been a great catch if he had made it with his glove."

"As far as I'm concerned," broadcaster John Lowenstein said, "it's the greatest catch of all time—because he didn't have a clue on that play."

Maybe the only person not overly impressed was pitcher Kevin Hickey. "It's a great catch," he admitted, but then claimed, "I've done that." But only when they were playing with a sixteen-inch softball, he added.

And the second only person not overly impressed with the catch was Mitchell's brother, D'Angelo Mitchell, who claimed, "He learned that from me." Of course, D'Angelo is currently playing wide receiver in college.

The two fielding events that probably got the most attention in 1989 were Mets shortstop Kevin Elster's record-breaking 88-game errorless streak, and catcher Benny Distefano catching. During Elster's long streak former Yankee shortstop/coach/scout/manager Gene Michael called him "the best shortstop I've seen as far as catching the ball. He's got such great hands and is always in position to field the ball. The best ever."

Naturally, Elster was extremely pleased when told of Michael's praise. "That's nice," he said, and then asked, "Who's Gene Michael?"

Elster established himself in '89 as the next great defensive shortstop in the National League when Ozzie Smith finally slows down—which Ozzie is showing no signs of doing. Even Elster admits that. When he was asked after his streak had ended, on a routine ground ball, if he thought he would ever take Ozzie's place as the NL's All-Star shortstop, he replied honestly, "Not until he's dead."

Pirates catcher Benny Distefano took his place in baseball history just by catching. The difference between Distefano and every other catcher in the big leagues in 1989 is that Distefano is left-handed. So when manager Jim Leyland put him in to catch the ninth inning during a loss to the Braves, Distefano became the first left-hander to catch in the big leagues since Mike Squire caught two games for the White Sox in 1980. The only other left-handed catcher in recent times was Dale Long, who caught two games for the Pirates in 1958. "We've been working with Distefano in the bullpen," Pirates coach Rich Donnelly said. "When he warms up, we put a full-length mirror in front of him, so he thinks he's right-handed. But he did okay in the game. He looked stupid; we were all laughing. There was one pitch he didn't catch; he captured."

"It ain't that easy," Distefano said after his inning behind the plate, "but it's helped keep me in the majors, and I want to stay here." Distefano started the game at first base, but was put behind the plate after Leyland had pinch-hit for his two real catchers. Pitcher Bill Landrum retired the side on a strikeout and two ground balls. Distefano had been prepared for his debut, having worked on catching for three weeks in Instructional League after the '88 season. "I'm glad it finally happened," he said, "but the bottom line is that we didn't win the game."

The truth is that Distefano probably wouldn't have been much worse behind the plate than the Pirates' second-string catcher, Junior Ortiz. Ortiz seems to be very honest about his own ability. When first-string catcher Mike LaValliere returned to the lineup after missing several games with an injury, Ortiz said, "I'm real happy about this—because now I won't play as much, and people won't be on my rear end every day. I'll make them suffer. Now they have to wait till I play."

Ortiz, who claimed he wanted to wear number 0 because "anytime you want to do anything, what do you do? You dial 0," once told reporters that he was a much better catcher at Dodger Stadium than at other ball parks because of the ground-level box seats at Dodgers' park. "You don't want a passed ball there," he explained, "because when you run back to the screen you are looking people right in the eye and they're saying, 'Ortiz, you are the worst.'"

Of course, sometimes it's hard to be certain that Ortiz knows exactly what he's saying. When he didn't start the first night game the Pirates had ever played in Wrigley Field, he said, "You want to know why I didn't start? Because I don't hit good here at night."

Maybe Ortiz really isn't as bad as he claims, but he could be and still be playing in the big leagues, as there is a definite shortage of capable catchers. When Baltimore' starting catcher, Mickey Tettleton, was hurt, the O's immediately signed free agent Jamie Quirk. That might not seem like such a drastic move, until it's pointed out that during Quirk's fifteen-year major league career he's been given his unconditional release nine different times. The Royals have released him on four different occasions. During '89 Quirk was released by the Yankees, signed by the first-place Oakland A's, released by Oakland, and signed by the then first-place Baltimore Orioles. As long as Quirk didn't have to play very much, he was a very valuable man to have on the team. It's only when he had to play that he wasn't that valuable, hitting .176 for three teams.

I think one of the reasons Quirk continues to find a job is that he's a good guy to have in the dugout. He tends to look at the world squatted down through iron bars. For example, after the Yankees had played an early-season game in very cold weather, he said, "As catcher, I'm probably least affected by the cold, but it would be nice to have Ken Kaiser umpiring behind me—he blocks more wind than other umpires."

The need for catchers got so acute at one point that the Mets, who began the '89 season with three catchers on their major league roster, had to type up an emergency contract for their bullpen catcher Rob Dromerhauser, who'd never appeared in a major league game. But before Dromerhauser was activated, help arrived from the minor leagues.

Most teams have players they call their "designated catchers," position players who would fill in behind the plate for a few innings in an emergency. The truth is, if some of those people actually had to catch, they'd be creating the emergency. It probably would be more appropriate to refer to them as "designated missers."

Baseball seems to run in cycles. For a time there are a lot of catchers, but no shortstops; then a scout discovers San Pedro de Macoris, in the Dominican Republic, the place where shortstops are born, and there's an abundance of good-fielding shortstops—but no catchers. Usually teams just move players around to fill their immediate needs, but few teams made as many position shifts as the Phillies did in '89. Their entire starting outfield—Juan Samuel, Chris James, and Von Hayes—had all started in their infield in '88. As pitcher Don Carman pointed out, "If anybody tries to steal center field, we got him."

A lot of teams had defensive problems in '89. Padres manager Jack McKeon admitted, for example, that his two third basemen, Tim Flannery and Randy Ready, really were "no Brooks Robinson." Flannery claimed that they were close: "We're actually the Brooks Brothers. You know, Foster and Mel."

Apparently McKeon was right. In the first Saturday night game ever played at Wrigley Field, the Padres and Cubs made a combined eleven errors. Flannery wasn't surprised, explaining, "You're just not supposed to play night games at Wrigley Field. You don't mess with tradition. This is what happens."

The game was played so badly that when the official scorer ruled that a ball hit at Ready by a Cubs batter was a base hit rather than an error, the crowd actually booed. "They wanted errors," Ready said afterward. "They wanted them bad."

And that's what they got, a lot of bad errors. The Cubs' All-Star second baseman, Ryne Sandberg, had only the third two-error game of his career, one being his first throwing error in almost two full seasons. Cub shortstop Shawon Dunston, who has one of the strongest throwing arms in baseball, threw a ball straight into the Padre dugout. McKeon said, "After that we thought we had all better wear our helmets in the dugout."

Don Zimmer summed up the evening for everyone when he said, flatly, "Worst big league game I've ever seen."

I guess 1989 was a tough year for all third basemen, not just Flannery and Ready. The First Worst Third Baseman of the Year Award goes to the Phillies' Charlie Hayes, who beat out a bad field by committing four errors in the first four innings in a game against Houston. Hayes's first two errors came in the first inning, when he fielded a bunt and threw the ball away, and then fielded a routine grounder and also threw that away. He misplayed a ground ball in the second inning and made another bad throw in the fourth inning. Hayes's four-no-star performance left safe the record for most errors by a player in one game, six, set in a thirteen-inning game by shortstop Bill O'Neill in 1904. The record for errors by an individual in a nine-inning game is five.

Hayes had a lot of competition for this award. Pirate third baseman Bobby Bonilla made twenty-six errors; ironically, six of them were made on ground balls hit to him by other third basemen. And the Mets' Howard Johnson had a terrible first half of the '89 season, during which every throw he made toward first base became an adventure. "HoJo," as he's often called in the New York papers, was dubbed "ThrowJo" by the *New York Post*. Johnson had a difficult time getting his arm back in condition after an off-season operation on his shoulder. "When you've had surgery," he explained, "you have to reeducate your muscles."

"Maybe," a reporter asked, "but do you have to start in kindergarten?"

The former Dodger third baseman Pedro Guerrero returned to his original position, first base, with the Cardinals in '89. Unfortunately, the results were not much better. Manager Whitey Herzog said that Guerrero juggled so many balls at first base that "every time somebody hits a ball to Pedro, it should be scored 3–3–3 unassisted."

Without doubt the Defensive Oddity of the Year Award goes to Ozzie Smith. In Ozzie's case, news is made not when he makes a great play but when he makes an error. Smith, generally considered the greatest fielding shortstop of all time, made errors on routine plays in two consecutive games, allowing the Pirates to win both of them.

The Pirates were strong contenders for the What the Lord Giveth Award. In addition to Bonilla at third base, they had Gary Redus, who played some first base for them. And it was some first base. One day Redus went after a high pop-up in foul territory. Just a routine foul pop-up. A playable pop-up. And Redus didn't come close to catching it. How much did he miss it by? Well, according to coach Rich Donnelly, "If that ball had been a hand grenade, Redus wouldn't have had anything to worry about."

It was also a tough year defensively for some outfielders—the Yankees' Mel Hall, for instance. The Yankees and A's were in a scoreless game in the sixth inning. With two outs and a runner on second, Oakland's Carney Lansford hit a routine fly ball to Hall in left field. The runner on second started jogging around third as Hall moved over to make the catch. "When I was running after it," Hall explained, "the sun wasn't in my eyes. But when I stopped, the ball went in the sun. I kept waiting for the sun to move. It never moved." Hall immediately went into the catcher's crouch, to try to change his angle on the ball, then he dropped to one knee, then he did the only sensible thing—he covered his head so the ball wouldn't hurt him. It dropped slightly behind him. "You hang in there as long as you can," he said; "after that, you have to bail."

Talking about the play a few days later, Hall, who is black, told reporters, "If I was white, I would have been red."

Andy Van Slyke also lost a fly ball in the sun, but he was much luckier, making an incredible over-the-shoulder catch. "Because of the sun, I didn't see the ball for the last twenty yards. I just put my glove up, plain and simple, and the ball landed in it. There may have been thirty thousand surprised people, but no one was more surprised than I was."

Waiting for the sun to move?

Hall wasn't the only Yankee outfielder to have fielding problems. In fact, Hall's greatest fear is exactly what happened to center fielder Roberto Kelly: he was hit on the head. Twice. In one week. Kelly is actually a pretty good fielder, and twice in that week he tried to make diving catches of line drives hit in front of him. And in both cases the ball took a short hop and conked him on the head. Luis Polonia, then with the A's, hit the first ball, and was out at home plate trying for an inside-the-park home-run. Ken Griffey, Jr., who hit the second one to hit Kelly, did receive credit for an inside-the-parker. Comparing the two hits, Kelly decided, "Griffey's bounced farther off my head...but it didn't hurt as much."

Jesse Barfield played right field for the Yankees most of the season, and he finished in a tie with the Mets' Darryl Strawberry for the Throw of the Year by a New York Right Fielder. After the Red Sox' Nick Esasky had hit a home run against New York at Yankee Stadium, the fans threw the ball back on the field. Barfield, frustrated after having struck out three times, just picked up the ball and threw it as far as he could—over the bleachers, over a huge Citibank sign, and onto Jerome Avenue. It was a place where no baseball had ever been hit, must less thrown. "It was just a way of getting rid of the frustration," Barfield said.

"He always had a great arm," Red Sox manager Joe Morgan said of the throw.

"He must have picked it up from me," reliever Dave Righetti said. In 1986, after giving up a grand slam home run to George Bell in Toronto, Righetti took the new ball given to him by the umpire and heaved it into the right-field bleachers.

Barfield was playing with the Blue Jays during that game and remembered Righetti's throw. "Mine didn't go as far," he decided.

Strawberry earned his part of the award during a game against the Padres. In the ball game he was 0 for 4, committed an error in right field, and was thrown out at the plate after running through the third base coach's stop sign. So when he caught a routine fly ball to end the eighth inning, he turned around and threw the ball over the right field fence, over 42 rows of seats, and into the parking lot. Strawberry refused to talk about that throw, but pitcher Ron Darling said, "Hopefully, it didn't hit anybody." Well, we know he missed the cutoff man. Unless the cutoff man was parking his car.

There must have been something strange happening in right field in 1989—besides the right fielders. Obviously the Tigers' Scott Lusader was the wrong person to have in right field—he tied a major league record by committing three errors in one inning, allowing the White Sox to score seven runs. Playing on a field that was soaked from an overnight storm, and in a game that started very late in the afternoon because it was being telecast, Lusader lost two fly balls in the sun for errors, then made a bad throw. Only seven other outfielders have committed three errors in one inning, and it was last done in the American League in 1925. "Somebody asked me if that was my worst nightmare," Lusader said after the game. "I told him, I've never dreamed of that and I hope I never do."

The Mets' Juan Samuel, who has played second base most of his career, played center field for the Phillies and Mets this season. As a center fielder, he admits he's a good second baseman. When Mark Parent lifted a routine fly ball to center, Samel, who was playing deep, came charging in, charging in, charging in, charging right past the spot where the ball landed, without ever touching it. "I kind of got a late break," he explained. "I saw the ball all the way. I just did one thing wrong—I didn't catch the SOB."

Sometimes, even when outfielders do exactly what they're supposed to do, they still have problems. The Expos' Otis Nixon, for example, fielded a one-hop single hit by Met Lee Mazzilli and came up throwing, trying to keep a runner on second from scoring—but his throw hit shortstop Spike Owen, who was standing about ten feet in front of him, right in the back. "I'm taking a lot of heat for it," Nixon said, "but it's a basic rule: hit the cutoff man. And that's what I did."

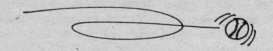

Great Stitions

When I was in the minor leagues I worked with an umpire who claimed he had absolutely no superstitions. None.

He walked under ladders, loved black cats, couldn't wait for Friday the thirteenth. But he kept an empty glass near the door, and he wouldn't leave our apartment unless he put a penny in that glass. Every time. When I asked him why he did that, he explained, "That's just to remind me not to be superstitious."

Because there is so much luck involved in the game of baseball—a pebble can turn a whole World Series around—baseball players are very careful to pay attention to the baseball gods. Among the many things Wade Boggs was known for before Margogate was the fact that he ate chicken before every game. Before every single game. Let me put it this way: if you went into a chicken's post office, you'd see a Wanted poster with Boggs's picture on it hanging right next to that of Frank Purdue. But Boggs certainly isn't the only player to follow his good taste. One of the biggest surprises of the '89 season was the emergence of Oriole catcher Mickey Tettleton as a legitimate big league slugger. Tettleton, a journeyman catcher until this season, hit 26 home runs for the O's. Where did this newfound power come from? "It could be the weightlifting," he said, "something I'd never done before in the off-season. Maybe the wind is blowing out." Then he admitted, "I have no idea."

But his wife, Sylvia, does. Fruit Loops. She said on TV that her husband had started eating Fruit Loops cereal before every day game. Oriole fans reacted by hanging a Fruit Loops banner from the upper deck in Tettleton's honor, then showered him with Fruit Loops confetti when he homered.

One man's Fruit Loops is another man's Hamburger Helper. The Pirates' Glenn Wilson found his strength at McDonald's. For one week, one magic week, pitchers couldn't get Wilson out. In 31 at bats, he hit .484, with 7 RBIs, 3 doubles, a triple, and 2 home runs. The reason:

the McDonald's Quarter-Pounder with Cheese, french fries, and a Coke that Wilson ate before every game. He was even late getting to the ball park one night because he had made a cab driver go out of the way to find a McDonald's. When a local McDonald's heard about this, the owner sent fifty Quarter-Pounders with Cheese to the Pirates' clubhouse for other players. Apparently, they didn't help anybody except Wilson—Wilson had three hits, the entire rest of the team had five more, as the Pirates lost to Houston.

And what does McDonald eat for good luck? Well, the night before the Orioles' Ben McDonald is scheduled to pitch he eats sardines—with mustard.

For several Yankees, the secret is raw sugar. Not eaten, just carried in their back pockets during the game. "I got a couple of hits and RBIs since I did it," Don Mattingly said. "So why not? And truthfully, raw sugar is supposed to make you stronger."

For ten straight pitching starts Bert Byleven ate meatballs and spaghetti before each game. And he won ten in a row. Then disaster struck: before his eleventh start he ate in an Italian restaurant that didn't serve meatballs. He tried, he ate pasta, but no meatballs. "I'm not superstitious," Byleven claimed, "but when things are going well you tend to do the same thing. But next time I go to a restaurant before I'm scheduled to pitch, I'm bringing my own meatballs."

Cleveland's Greg Swindell goes to the mound with a slightly different taste in his mouth—his fingernail. When Swindell is pitching he bites off a fingernail and stores it in his cheek during the game. "In college, I tried gum and didn't have any success. And I've always been afraid that if I dip tobacco, I'll swallow it."

Obviously, superstitions are not limited to food. Seattle's Randy Johnson prepares to pitch by listening to the soothing tunes of the heavy metal rock groups Metallica and Mötley Crüe.

After outfielder Luis Polonia saw the movie *Major League,* in which a slugger got his power from a voodoo doll, Polonia bought a doll of his own. He calls it Joe Vu "because that was the name of the doll in the movie. He got good luck with it; so will I." Polonia kept the doll in his locker, and before every game he put a small cup of hot coffee in front of it, stuck a cigarette in its mouth, and rubbed its head. Why did Polonia have to rub its head? "I don't know why," he admitted, "I just know you have to."

Mariners pitcher Brian Holman isn't really superstitious, but like a lot of players he usually says a brief prayer before a game. One night, though, after the Mariners had lost six straight, he was a little more direct. "Usually I just said, 'Lord, give me the strength and confidence to get the job done.' Tonight I said, 'Lord, I need a win.'" Holman gave up only five hits in six innings to beat Boston and end the losing streak.

The Cubs' Mitch Williams had a lot of close shaves in '89—but very few of them came in the bathroom. "I'm trying to get away with shaving only four times this season," he explained. "After my first 11 saves, I shaved. After my next 11 saves, I shaved." Asked if that meant his goal was 44 saves, he replied, "I just go out and play." Williams finished the season with 36 saves, or three-and-a-cheek shaves.

The Mets' Dwight Gooden also shaved only once this season—but he was shaving all the hair off his head. Gooden isn't superstitious, however. He did it, he explained, "because the Mets wanted me to lose weight."

Yankee rookie catcher Bob Geren also cut all the hair off his head—but that was a proposition rather than a superstition: he said he'd do it if the Yanks won six straight games. After their sixth consecutive win, Geren was shaved so bald that Steve Sax decided, "Stick two fingers in his nose, one in his mouth, and you could bowl 300."

Ladies' Daze

Sometimes I think that the only combination more dangerous than a woman and a baseball player is a woman and a good lawyer. That lesson was learned in 1989 by Wade Boggs, Steve Garvey, Dave Winfield, Darryl Strawberry, and Luis Polonia.

Wade Boggs's four-year affair with a woman named Margo Adams burst onto the sports pages when Margo broke up their relationship because he was seeing other women. She then sued him for $100,000, claiming he'd promised to compensate her for lost wages if she'd leave her job in real estate and travel with him on Red Sox road trips. Boggs responded by contacting the FBI and claiming she was trying to extort money from him. In response, she filed a $12 million lawsuit against him. Boggs never denied the affair, just that he'd promised to pay her.

Penthouse magazine paid Margo $100,000 to tell the inside story of her life on the road with a big leaguer, and how women are exploited by men—then take off all her clothes and pose nude for the magazine.

In *Penthouse*, Margo quoted Boggs as making several derogatory remarks about his teammates. She also claimed she helped him at bat. "One night," she wrote, "I went to the game and he went 4 for 5. He found out that I hadn't worn panties underneath my dress. So for the next couple of months, when he went into a slump, he'd ask me not to wear panties to the game."

As a T-shirt sold in Boston read: ".356 lifetime average. And you thought it was the chicken."

Well, maybe it was just the chick. After the story became public, fans in ball parks around the American League were very sympathetic to Boggs. And Khadafy is going to open a Carvel stand in Peoria. When the Red Sox played in Kansas City, a local radio station handed out cardboard cutouts of Margo's face mounted on wooden sticks. Whenever Boggs came to bat, the fans would hold up their masks and chant, "Mar-go, Margo." There was no comment on what they did with their undergarments to make him feel at home, however.

Boston fans actually were supportive of Boggs. On Opening Day they gave him several standing ovations to show their feelings. "It really meant the world to me," Boggs said. "I've been waiting all winter for this day. I didn't know what it was going to be like." Of course, the same fans who cheered Boggs booed Roger Clemens for remarks he'd made about Boston being a difficult city in which to raise a family. "That's up to the fans," manager Joe Morgan said about the two reactions, then added, "All I know is that they clapped for me."

While the case was in court, and the story was in *Penthouse*, Margo refused most requests for interviews. But she did respond to the *Boston Globe*'s Dan Shaughnessey when he asked her, "Have you lost some weight?" After she admitted that she had lost weight, Shaughnessey asked her if she was sick.

"No," she said, "I'm not trying to lose weight. Everybody already saw me nude. I'm probably the only person that ever posed nude—and then lost weight."

During this whole scandal there were persistent rumors that the Red Sox were trying to trade Boggs, while at the same time having difficulty trying to sign him to a new contract. Boggs said he wanted to stay in Boston, then added, correctly, "My contract is the least of my worries."

By the end of the '89 season the attorneys for Boggs and Adams were rumored to be negotiating a settlement; Boggs and his wife, Debbie, were together and happy; and Margo said she'd learned an important lesson: "My new motto is just say no to adultery."

George Brett is quite confident fans won't soon forget the story. "Look at me," he said. "It's been nine years since the hemorrhoid thing [in the 1980 World Series] and I still hear about it. The Pine Tar Incident was in 1983, and I still hear fans yelling about it. I'm sure he'll never hear the end of it."

Incidentally, Boggs was so shaken by the publicity that his average fell to only .330 from his lifetime average of .356.

The only other major leaguer Margo admitted having an affair with, before Boggs, was Steve Garvey. The fact that she'd been associated with two such great players was not lost on Tommy Lasorda, who saw her charms as lucky ones. "If one of my guys gets into a slump this season," he decided, "I'll just have to send him to Margo."

Garvey learned in 1989 that honesty pays—particularly if you're admitting paternity. The former Dodgers and Padres star was divorced from his wife, Cyndy, who has become a well-known television personality, several years ago. This past year he impregnated a woman in Atlanta, to whom he was engaged, impregnated a woman in San Diego, to whom he was not engaged, then married a woman who was not pregnant. "What's he trying to do?" Tommy Lasorda asked, in one of the more printable jokes told about Garvey's situation, "become the father of our country?"

Appearing on Larry King's TV interview show, Garvey said he would "step up to the plate" and accept full responsibility for the children, to which Roger McDowell suggested, "Hey, Steve, push that plate away once in a while."

Naturally, the big rumor going around was that Pete Rose had bet on Garvey in the Breeder's cup.

One person not laughing was Garvey's former wife, Cyndy. According to the book she wrote, *The Secret Life of Cyndy Garvey*, her former husband was no Wade Boggs. "Many nights, with Steve sleeping beside me, I lay awake for hours," she wrote. "At two or three in the morning, I'd go out into the living room and sit with Duffy the dog."

Dave Winfield is appealing a jury's decision that a common-law marriage existed between him and the mother of his daughter in Houston, Texas. In the trial the jury found that Winfield's four-year relationship with this woman fulfilled the Texas definition of a marriage and that she was legally entitled to as much as half his earnings since 1982.

Darryl Strawberry was also the subject of a paternity suit, and Luis Polonia was convicted of having sex with an underage girl he'd met at the ball park in Milwaukee.

There are a lot of things I'm perfectly willing to make jokes about. But none of them are these. I would bet, though, that there are a lot of big league baseball players who can't wait to get back on the playing field—where it's safe.

I just wouldn't bet Pete Rose.

Bo Knows Blows

When I was in college, some people said I was in a class
by myself. But that was mostly because nobody would
sit next to me in the classroom. Bo Jackson really does
seem to be in a class by himself. Not only did he hit one
of the longest home runs of the 1989 season, in the All-
Star Game, and not only did he convince dubious sports
fans that he could play—and star—in both professional
baseball and football, he also starred in the Sports Commercial of the Year. First seen accompanying rhythm and
blues legend Bo Diddley on the guitar, Bo is shown playing baseball, football, and basketball, bike racing, running track... And after each vignette, a star of that sport
says, "Bo knows football," or "Bo knows basektball,"
or bike racing, or all the other sports. Bo is also seen on
hockey skates, but Wayne Gretzky, instead of claiming,
"Bo knows hockey," wordlessly shakes his head from
side to side.

Finally, at the end of the commercial, Bo is seen attempting to play a wild riff on his guitar. And then Bo
Diddley frowns and says, "Bo don't know diddley."

There are an awful lot of people who would disagree
with that. "Bo is not just anybody," George Brett said
after Jackson had made a perfect 300-foot throw, flat-
footed, from the base of the outfield wall to home plate
to nail a runner trying to score the winning run in the
tenth inning of a game. "He's a super human being."

"I was the one thrown out," the Mariners' Harold Reynolds said. "I've seen it on replay, and I still don't believe it."

After a Detroit batter had smashed a line drive up the alley off Royals pitcher Mark Gubicza, "I turned around and thought, 'There's only one person in the world who can make that catch,'" Gubicza said, "'and fortunately, we've got that guy.'"

"The guy's awesome," Kirby Puckett said after the All-Star Game. "He almost blew out my shoulder just giving me a high five."

The first time the Twins' right-hander Rick Aguilera faced Jackson, the Royals had a runner on third and a left-handed batter on deck. Aguilera walked Jackson intentionally, explaining, "I'd seen him on television commercials and ESPN. That was enough."

Of course, there are always dissenters. The Angels' Devon White, who played against Bo in a Superstars competition, wasn't particularly impressed with his basketball ability, complaining, "All he can do is go up, knock you down, and dunk."

Sounds like a pro player to me.

The showpiece of Bo's 1989 season was his "Bohemoth" 448-foot home run to dead center field leading off the All-Star Game for the American League. "When he hit it, we were cheering," said the National League's Jay Howell. "We were sitting around slapping hands and saying, 'Geez, were you gonna pitch him?'"

Jackson himself was modest about the blast, claiming, "I just got a little piece of it."

The scary part is that he might not be kidding. Jackson just might be the strongest player in baseball history. A lot of players broke bats during the season—but not too many broke them over their own bodies. Bo broke two over his knee, one on his thigh, and one on his own head. Okay, he only cracked the one he hit himself over the head with.

Bo also had a great year as a running back for Al Davis's Los Angeles Raiders, becoming one of the few athletes in history to play two professional sports in one season—and the first player to star in both sports. Philadelphia Eagles coach Buddy Ryan said, "If I was Bo Jackson's father and he hit a baseball like he does, I wouldn't let him play against the Philadelphia Eagles. I'd keep him hitting home runs." Of course, he said that just before Jackson was to play against the Eagles.

"I know I can do both sports," Jackson said. "There's nothing physical about it. It's all mental. They ask me if I get tired. On my off-days, I'm up at seven-thirty, making myself do something to stay busy. At two-thirty in the afternoon, I'm wishing I was at the ball park. I'll get tired when I get old."

Asked if he might give up either baseball or football, he finally admits there is something Bo doesn't know, saying "Who knows? I might just give up both sports and play cricket. I could if I wanted to."

Like most well-publicized athletes, Bo gets letters from fans asking him for everything from an autograph to money. He estimates he receives as much as twenty pounds of mail a week. But even that isn't too much for him. "I'm a speed reader," he says.

Bo knows reading.

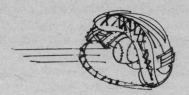

Little Bo's Peep

One other athlete played major league baseball and professional football in 1989, "Neon" Deion "Prime Time" Sanders, who played for the New York Yankees and Atlanta Falcons. And "Prime Time" claims he's not at all impressed by Jackson. "I think I can do anything," the flamboyant Sanders told reporters. "I could play for the Lakers if I had a chance. I get tired of hearing Bo's name. The only thing Bo has on me is age."

Upon hearing Sanders's remarks, Bo responded, "Deion should shut his mouth. Deion should take some advice: Like someone said, it's better to sit, look, and listen and be thought of as a fool, than to open your mouth and remove all doubt." Later Jackson added, "That's enough about him. That's enough small talk."

But 1989 was quite a year for Sanders, the Falcons' number one choice in the draft and a prized baseball prospect. He started the baseball season by creating a sensation when he reported to spring training—a day later than expected and draped in so much gold jewelry that one Yankee remarked, "He must watch a lot of the Home Shopping Network."

He immediately alienated some of his teammates when he objected to being given a high uniform number, saying, "Big numbers are for players people don't know."

When a reporter asked him about his gold chains, including two that had large dollar signs hanging from them, and another that had "Prime Time" on the end, he explained, "You dress good, you feel good. You feel good, you play good. You play good, they pay good."

Most people suspected that Sanders, unlike Jackson, was really using his baseball talent as leverage to get the football contract he wanted. Sanders didn't deny that, but claimed, "Right now I'm thinking only about baseball and trying to learn as much as I can. I'm a star in football, but in baseball I'm just a scab."

Sanders struggled for a time in the minor leagues, at one point being fined fifty dollars by his manager for showing up late at the ball park. "I only missed two minutes of stretching for the double-header," he complained. "Every clock in the hotel was thirty minutes slow. Most of the guys show up three hours early, that's why they were on time."

Sanders was demanding one of the largest contracts in pro football history from the Falcons, slightly more than $10 million. "I just want it to rhyme with my name— Deion, million." But when the football season started, Sanders was still playing baseball. He never forgot his objective, though—most players put their uniform numbers on the knob of their bat with a Magic Marker; Sanders identified his bats with a dollar sign.

When several Yankee outfielders were injured, George Steinbrenner decided to promote Sanders to the big leagues, and he performed creditably. "Football is my life," Sanders had said; "baseball is my girlfriend." But after he'd played his first big league game his agent, Steve Zucker, said, "The girlfriend just became Miss America."

Playing for the Yankees made Sanders think quite differently about a career in baseball. "Right now baseball's still my hobby," he said, "but that's changing every day. I want to be rich and happy. I just don't want to be rich."

The Falcons finally made him rich, signing him to a four-year, $4.5 million contract. On a Wednesday evening, Sanders left a Columbus Clippers game in the sixth inning and flew to Atlanta; the following Sunday he was returning punts for the Falcons. On his second play in professional football he ran 68 yards for a touchdown. "I thought they had me bottled up," he said after the game, "But once I got outside, it's prime time from there, and I said, 'What have I done?'"

Watching Sanders's performance on the gridiron, Lou Piniella said, "It just goes to show that baseball players are superior athletes and in great shape."

And Bucky Dent added with admiration, "He's faster than a hiccup."

Because Sanders left in the middle of the baseball season, unlike Jackson, he became the first athlete in history to hit a home run in the major leagues and score a touchdown in the NFL in the same week. Jim Thorpe did it twice, but he scored his touchdowns in the American Professional Football League, the forerunner of the NFL.

Jackson and Sanders aren't the only athletes to try to play two pro sports. The Minnesota Vikings' running back D. J. Dozier worked out with the Mets in spring training and said, after hitting .312, with a home run, 12 RBIs, and 9 stolen bases, "I definitely feel I demonstrated to myself that I can play pro baseball, and that's very satisfying. I know I can play better."

Maybe, but can he read twenty pounds of letters a week?

All-Pro punt returner Bobby Joe Edmonds played center field in '89 for the Double A Reading, Pennsylvania, Phillies. In his first year of pro ball, Edmonds hit only .198 in 101 at bats. But when Deion Sanders came to Reading with the Albany Yankees, the two of them had lunch to discuss the difficulty of trying to play two sports. "I told him," Edmonds said, "that whatever happens, to keep believing in himself—and that's something Deion doesn't have any trouble doing."

Probably the major league team most suited for a football game would be the St. Louis Cardinals—who had three former college punters on the team at the same time. So, as one sportswriter suggested, all Whitey Herzog needs is a capable long snapper.

As long as they're not punting to the Yankees' Deion Sanders.

A Medium Well-Equipped

As I've mentioned, for a brief time I owned a sporting goods store. I wasn't very good at it, however. I carried things like bats that floated. But the experience did make me more aware than ever of the importance of good equipment—and a good accountant. Obviously, the most important piece of baseball equipment is the baseball. Well, at least most of the time. Before an early season game the Orioles took infield practice without a ball. They went through all the motions and played almost flawlessly. Cal Ripkin did bobble one, but it took a bad hop. "We've been on the road so long," general manager Roland Hemond said, "we're barnstorming."

The only significant difference in the baseball this year was that the National League ball carried the signature of the league's new president, Bill White. After the Cubs had hit six home runs during a game at Busch Stadium, a stunned Whitey Herzog said, "I think that's a record for this park. Pittsburgh and the Giants each hit five once. It's funny, I was going to check before the game to see whether the balls were dead. We just got a shipment of Bill White balls in. Maybe that made a difference."

Certainly the strangest glove seen in the major leagues in 1989 was the reversible model used by the Phillies' ambidextrous reliever Greg Harris. When Harris was brought into a game against the Pirates and Andy Van Slyke, who was on third base, saw the glove, he asked third baseman Randy Ready about it. Ready told him that Harris used it "because he's amphibious."

"Oh," Van Slyke said; "does that mean he can pitch underwater?"

Padres third baseman Tim Flannery is one of the few players in the big leagues still using an old leather glove, on which he's written "Anti-Greenhouse Glove." Asked about the glove, Flannery explained, "Because of the greenhouse effect, they've had to give cows steroids. That's why the leather on the old gloves is better than the leather on the new ones."

The controversy between wood bats and aluminum bats continued in 1989. With colleges using only aluminum bats, some people are beginning to suspect that metal bats might someday be used in professional baseball. In a typical year, according to USA Today, a major league team uses slightly more than 2,000 bats a season at a cost of $35,000. Two dozen aluminum bats, costing about $1,500, would serve for the whole season. The problem is that the baseball comes off the metal bat much faster, and with much greater force. "The day they use aluminum bats is the day I retire," pitcher Greg Minton said. "I've already wounded enough first basemen and third basemen with hanging sliders."

Ken Griffey, Jr., laughed at the thought of putting metal bats into the hands of such powerful hitters as Alvin Davis, Jose Canseco, Mark McGwire, and Bo Jackson. "First you'd better give everybody life insurance, because someone will get killed."

Tim Flannery thought it was possible, "but only if they get a softer baseball."

And Braves shortstop Andres Thomas actually thought it was a good idea, saying "I'd be a home run hitter."

Toronto's Rance Mullinicks remained neutral. "I don't know anything about aluminum bats," he admitted, "but they make great fishing poles."

The controversy got so lukewarm that Representative Richard Durbin (D-Ill) stood up for wood in the House of Representatives, proclaiming passionately, in the hallowed chambers once graced by Abraham Lincoln, "Baseball fans have been forced to endure countless indignities by those who just cannot leave well enough alone. Designated hitters, plastic grass, uniforms that look like pajamas, chicken clowns dancing on the base lines, and, of course, the most heinous sacrilege, lights in Wrigley Field.

"Are we willing to hear the crack of the bat replaced by the dinky ping? Are we ready to see the Louisville Slugger replaced by the aluminum ping dinger? Is nothing sacred?...What is next? Teflon baseballs? Radar-enhanced gloves? I ask you.

"I do not want to hear about saving trees. Any tree in America would gladly give its life for the glory of a day at home plate..."

"I do not know if it will take a constitutional amendment to keep baseball traditions alive, but if we forsake the great Americana of broken-bat singles and pine tar, we will have certainly lost our way as a nation."

Beautiful, beautiful, except for the part where he talks about the crack of the bat. If the bat didn't crack so easily, this issue wouldn't even exist.

Steve Sax, like most major leaguers, is very satisfied with wooden bats. Using a new wooden bat one night, he went 5 for 5. Treating that bat with the respect it had earned, instead of leaving it in the bat rack, he decided to keep it in his locker. But as he was putting it away, he noticed a blue smear on it. When he looked more closely, that blue smear turned out to be the reverse signature of Dr. Bobby Brown, the former surgeon now serving as American League president, whose signature appears on every AL baseball. Manager Dallas Green immediately realized what had happened, pointing out, "It must be a doctored bat."

Among the things that aren't uniform in baseball are uniforms. They come in different sizes, colors, and materials—not to mention the numbers on the backs—and almost every player wears his uniform in his own special way. When the Toronto Blue Jays were given their new uniforms for the 1989 season, for example, manager Jimy Williams was asked what he liked best about them. His answer was obvious. "I got one," he said.

One player who had 1988 AL Cy Young Award winner Frank Viola's number was Dwight Gooden. And that number was 16. Both Viola and Gooden had worn it throughout their big league careers, which created a problem when Viola was traded to the Mets. Gooden politely explained how relatively unimportant a uniform number is to a player when he said, "Frank can have my wife, use my locker, I'll take him out for dinner, but no way am I giving up my number."

I guess Viola's decision would probably depend on what number Gooden's wife had.

Rickey Henderson had a similar problem when he was traded to the A's and discovered that catcher Ron Hassey was wearing number 24, which Henderson has worn throughout his career. "What's a number anyway?" Hassey asked. "Just something you stick on your back so people will know who you are." He asked that just before he accepted $2,500 in stereo equipment from Henderson to give up the number.

Traditionally, regular players wear low numbers while rookies get very high numbers. When Steve Sax reported to the Yankees, he asked for number 3. That was Babe Ruth's number, he was reminded, and it had been retired. When Sax ran into his old manager, Tommy Lasorda, he told him the story, then said, "They won't give me Babe's number. Man, he can't use it."

The Yankees have retired so many low numbers once worn by great players in their history that if they keep using fifty players a season, they're eventually going to run out of numbers. In 1989, for example, six different players wore number 28 during the season, four players wore 34, and numbers 18, 22, 26, 33, and 54 were each worn by three different players. "From 1990 on," Rafael Santana said, "the Yankees are going to have uniform numbers 101 and up."

The uniform number given to a young player really is an indication of how much the team thinks of his ability. For example, in spring training Red Sox pitcher Gene Harris wore number 61, but when he made the team he was given number 43. To him, that meant only one thing. "I'm no longer a pulling guard," he said happily.

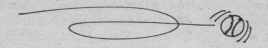

If Records Really Are Made to Be Broken, No Wonder They Invented Cassette Tapes

In terms of breaking records, 1989 was not a record-breaking year. Probably the two most important record-breaking peformances were Nolan Ryan topping his own career strikeout record with his more than 5,000 strike-outs, and relief pitcher Kent Tekulve smashing Hoyt Wilhelm's record for appearances when he pitched in his 1,019th game. Teke pointed out that his longevity had nothing to do with exercise or running. "What's the point in running ten miles," he asked, "just to get back to the point where you started?"

In a record-barren season, the Mets' Kevin Elster went 88 games without making an error at shortstop, to break the old record. Before his 89th game the Mets gave him a trophy for his achievement—and when the game started, Elster threw away the first ball hit to him for an error.

Fielding records simply don't generate the excitement of, say, pit-spitting for distance. Most people noticed when Ryne Sandberg set a record for errorless games at second base, but no one even realized that catcher Rick Cerone had broken Yogi Berra's record of playing 148 consecutive errorless games until he had reached 157. Naturally, two games after Cerone was informed he had the record, he dropped a foul pop-up for an error.

Here's another record those whacky statisticians somehow missed. When Astros outfielder Terry Puhl played in his 1,424th major league game, he broke the old record for most games played by a Canadian-born player, which had been set between 1908 and 1922 by the Indians' Jack Graney. Puhl's teammate Craig Reynolds felt he at least deserved honorable mention, claiming he should get credit for Most Years Rooming with a Canadian. (10).

And the California Angels proudly announced that they'd set a new team record for the number of times a home game was interrupted by a beach ball bouncing on the field. The old record of 532 was shattered, but an independent auditor is currently reviewing the tapes to verify a new record.

Some very important records were tied in '89. Nolan Ryan became only the sixth pitcher in big league history to beat all twenty-six teams during the regular season, a record that will stand at least until expansion. Ryan joined Doyle Alexander, Gaylord Perry, Don Sutton, Mike Torrez, and Rick Wise in the select group. Tommy John also beat every team, but some of his wins came in postseason games.

Braves relief pitcher Paul Assermacher became only the twentieth pitcher in history to strike out four batters in an inning. The Indians' Joe Carter became the fifteenth player to hit five home runs in two consecutive games and tied Lou Gehrig's AL record with the fourth three-homer game of his career. Dale Murphy became the fourteenth player to hit two home runs in one inning and the tenth to knock in six runs in an inning. Yankee pitchers Dale Mohorcic and Andy Hawkins hit a total of four batters in a game, becoming the first Yankee pitchers to accomplish that feat since 1921. Blue Jays rookie Junior Felix, who had homered on the first pitch thrown to him in Triple A baseball in April, homered on the first pitch thrown to him in the big leagues a month later—becoming the fifty-third player in history to do that—and guaranteeing that from that point on, his entire career is going downhill.

With six doubles in two straight games, Kirby Puckett tied twelve other players for most doubles in two games. I told you it wasn't much of a record-breaking year.

The Mets broke the National League record and tied the major league mark by playing an entire game without recording one assist in the field. Of the 27 putouts, they recorded 13 strikeouts, the catcher caught 3 pop-ups, infielders caught 3 pop-ups, outfielders caught 6 fly balls, and 2 unassisted put-outs were recorded at first base.

Some very important streaks continued or were ended in '89. Dodger pitcher Orel Hershiser's major league record of 59 consecutive scoreless innings set in '88 ended in the first inning he pitched in '89, when the Reds scored a run. The Yankees won a game on the day infielder Wayne Tolleson's son was born, continuing a streak begun in 1977 of always winning on the day a member of the team has a baby. Don Mattingly decided, "We're going to have to find a bunch of surrogate mothers." It seems to me it would be a lot easier just to sign Steve Garvey.

Pirates pitching coach Ray Miller's team won on his birthday for the seventh straight season. And the Orioles' Cal Ripken's consecutive inning streak ended at 1,003, when umpire Drew Coble ejected him for arguing a call. Afterward, a very sad Coble admitted, "I felt like I'd just thrown God out of Sunday school."

In the "What a Difference a Year Makes" category, the Pirates' Bob Walk had been the last starting pitcher to give up a home run in 1988, throwing 103⅓ innings before someone took him deep. The second batter he faced in '89 hit a home run off him. Rafael Palmeiro batted 580 times in '88 without being credited with one game-winning RBI. Even though that statistic was officially eliminated, Palmeiro knocked in the winning run in his third '89 game. The Padres won the first game of every home stand in '88; naturally, they lost the first game of their first home stand in '89. In the first week of the '89 season, Pirates shortstop Rafael Belliard, who'd set a major league record for most at bats (286) without a double, doubled. And finally, by the end of April 1989, Jack Morris, the winningest pitcher in baseball in the 1980s, and Frank Viola, who won more games than any other pitcher between 1984 and 1988, were a combined 0–10.

In addition to these substantial marks, some unusual occurrences took place in '89. The Braves' veteran catcher Bruce Benedict completed a rare triple-triple when he finally hit into a triple play, after previously being involved in triple plays as a catcher and a base runner.

Minnesota's Randy Bush joined an elite group of players in 1989 when he hit his first home run, becoming one of the very few people with the same last name as the incumbent President of the United States to hit a home run in a major league game. The last player to accomplish this was Gary Carter, who hit 102 home runs while Jimmy Carter was in the White House. Before that, outfielder Dan Ford had slugged 35 home runs while Gerald Ford was in office, Deron Johnson had 98 round-trippers in the Lyndon Johnson years, and infielder John Kennedy had one home run while John F. Kennedy was running the country. I suspect Phil Bradley might be looking forward to the 1992 presidential elections, while Steve Kemp, currently playing in the Senior League, might be thinking about making a comeback.

And, for the record, the Last of the Best in 1989 was Cubs outfielder Darrin Jackson—assuming that the players on the major league rosters at the start of the season are the best baseball players in America. Jackson was the last of the players who opened the 1989 season in the big leagues to appear in a box score. Sixteen games into the season, manager Don Zimmer finally used him as a pinch-runner. Jackson didn't even threaten the record set in 1982 by Red Sox catcher Roger LaFrancois, who didn't appear in a game until May 27.

He Drives Me Crazy

Baseball's biggest slugger, the A's Jose Canseco, was in the headlines all season for just about everything except baseball. Canseco's problems behind the steering wheel made him America's best-known driver since Ralph Kramden; his broken wrist kept him out of the lineup for more than half the season; he set up a profit-making telephone line so fans could find out important information such as what he had for breakfast—and then, in the playoffs, he made fans remember why they cared in the first place.

Canseco's driving problems began before spring training, when he was ticketed in Florida for driving 125 mph in his candy-apple-red Jaguar, although Canseco claimed that that was inaccurate—he was only going 120.

Three weeks after that, he was stopped by Phoenix, Arizona, police for going through a red light, failing to produce his driver's license or proof of insurance, and having improper license plates on the car. Canseco said the tickets were "totally uncalled for, totally unnecessary," and claimed the ticketing officers were "very mechanical, very cold, very strict, by the book. I mean, have a heart."

It was at this point that Canseco began to suspect his red Jaguar was attracting attention. "I've been thinking," he said, "maybe I should ride a ten-speed from now on, or maybe I'll get a horse."

Instead of a horse, he got something much more conservative—a white Porsche convertible. But even that new image didn't help him: he was cited in California for driving 51 mph in a 35 mph zone. The officer who stopped him said he thought Canseco was actually going faster, but he couldn't get a correct radar reading. When someone asked Canseco if he'd been for the infraction, he asked, with surprise, "Me? Not get a ticket?"

Finally, after getting all those tickets, Canseco decided he should buy a boat, pointing out, "There's no speed limit on the water."

When Jose reported for spring training, manager Tony LaRussa noticed that one of his wrists looked bigger than the other, and asked him what kind of workouts he'd been doing. Canseco told him, "All I've been doing all winter is pulling out my driver's license."

The fact is that Canseco's wrist was fractured, and when the season opened he was on the disabled list, since he needed an operation on the wrist. Ironically, his twin brother, Ozzie, a player in the A's minor league system, had had exactly the same operation performed on his wrist in '88. Now, I've heard that baldness can be inherited, and a weight problem, and blue eyes...but weak wrists? Who ever heard somebody say, "I got my wrists from my father's side?" One sportswriter noted that Canseco's broken wrist would keep him out of action until the All-Star Game—and presumably prevent him from driving at Indianapolis.

While Canseco was visiting a doctor in San Francisco, police found a loaded semiautomatic handgun on the floor of his car. Some guys just have bad luck, tickets, a broken wrist, a semiautomatic handgun on the floor of their car. Jose was detained by the police again. I've never seen anybody spend that much time with the police and not qualify for a pension.

Canseco said that the gun was licensed in another state and he was carrying it for protection because both he and his wife had been threatened.

Although Canseco didn't play an inning the first half of the season, fans still voted him into the American League All-Star team. He didn't play in the game either. But a few days later he returned to the A's lineup. In his first game back he homered and stole a base, leading Royals manager John Wathan to point out, "He's only played one game and he's already in the one-and-one club."

Finally, Canseco decided to tell his side of all the problems he'd had—but instead of talking to reporters, he went directly to the fans. Especially the fans with Touchtone telephones. When he was arrested on the gun charge, he complained, "I've been getting a lot of threats at home the past few weeks. Everyone gets my number. I don't know where everyone gets my number. I have to change my number periodically."

Somewhere along the line he must have changed his mind, because he changed his phone number to 1-900-234-JOSE, and to call him it costs two dollars the first minute, a dollar a minute after that. And he started advertising the number on television. "Hi, I'm Jose Canseco," his commercials began, "I want to speak to you...I'll give you the latest scoop on baseball and what's happening in my life. If you want to know if I take steroids, how fast I drive, or why I was carrying that gun, call me at 1-900-234-JOSE..."

After Tony LaRussa had seen the commercial, he admitted, "I thought, 'This is ridiculous.' It'll be interesting to see where he got the advice to do it. Maybe he took his own advice."

"How it originally came out was, the media stuff was happening with the speeding and the guns," Canseco said, "and people weren't getting the story from the horse's mouth." Each day Jose recorded a new message, revealing inside information like: "Me and my wife sat at home and watched body-building on TV. Esther got up on the bed and started flexing. Let me tell you, she's pretty built." On another day, Jose advised young callers, "Listen to your parents if they make sense, but don't listen to them if they're crazy."

One person who certainly didn't call was teammate Terry Steinbach, who said, "I hear enough of him during the course of a day. I don't want to hear him on the telephone."

The Blue Jays' Mookie Wilson knew how Jose felt about having people call him at home. Mookie said he does not like to give people his home number. "No one knows that. I don't even know that," he claimed.

Playing only half a season, Canseco hit .269, with 17 home runs and 57 RBIs, to help the A's win their second straight division title. In the fourth game of the AL playoffs against Toronto, Canseco reminded everyone why fans find him so interesting. He blasted a home run an estimated 480 feet into the upper deck of the Skydome, more than 70 feet above the field. "The last time I saw one hit that far," teammate Mark

McGwire said, "I was watching Greg Norman on the first tee."

Oakland outfield Billy Beane said, "It was of biblical proportions."

Catcher Ernie Whitt was suitably impressed, saying proudly, "I've never called a pitch that went that far."

And, naturally, Jose Canseco was his usual, humble self, saying modestly, "Just missed it."

Men of the Calling

Once again in 1989, the umpires of both the American and National League had a sensational year. Every one of them went through the entire season, including the regular season, playoffs, and World Series, without making a wrong call. They handled every game perfectly, kept control of even the most difficult situations on the field, dealt compassionately with deranged managers, and stayed happily and contentedly in the background.

Maybe you expected something different?

As I've said many times, being an umpire is like standing between two seven-year-olds holding one ice cream cone. No matter what decision an umpire makes, 50 percent of all the people involved are going to be sure he's wrong. Jose Canseco, for example, insisted that umpire John Hirshbeck was wrong to eject him from a September game. "That's the first time I've been thrown out of a game in my career," he said. "He can probably put a feather in his cap and feel good about it."

The next day the A's were playing in Cleveland, and a new umpiring crew was working the game. But when Canseco came onto the field, one of the first people he saw was third base umpire Drew Coble—who had a feather stuck in his cap.

The 1989 season started calmly enough for umpires when the NL's Bob Davidson threw out three Pirates for fighting in a spring training game. The three, R. J. Reynolds, Barry Bonds, and Bobby Bonilla, coincidentally wore numbers 23, 24, and 25. Or, maybe not coincidentally, as Davidson claimed, "It just makes it easier for the fans."

The season included the normal number of arguments and ejections and arguments about ejections. After AL umpire Greg Kosc had ejected Jim Dwyer for touching him twice during an argument, Twins manager Tom Kelly complained, "If that's considered bumping, maybe we ought to be playing in skirts."

Even Whitey Herzog got the boot for the first time in more than two seasons. Whitey was quite upset about it, claiming, "I was trying to break Lou Gehrig's record."

Pete Rose tried to be understanding when Eric Gregg, who is a large man, a large, large man, threw Reds pitcher Tom Browning out of a game. "Eric was in a bad mood," Pete said. "He probably didn't get a late breakfast.

One of the biggest arguments of the '89 season took place after Doug Rader's Angels had lost a game to the Orioles in Baltimore because of a disputed home run call—a few days after Frank Robinson had threatened to quit because the umpires were against him. Rader was irate that Jim McKean's crew had ruled a long drive by the O's Mike Devereaux a fair ball. Rader was still so angry a day after the call was made that he was ejected before the next game started. He went up to home plate for the pregame meeting, looked at the Orioles' starting lineup card, and told the umpires, "There are four names missing. Yours." After being warned that he was close to being ejected, Rader said, "You can get me now, or you can get me later. You might as well get me now, because eventually you're going to screw up and I'll be all over you."

That wasn't an ejection, that was an invitation. Rader really should have gotten an assist on that one. The *Washington Post*'s Tony Kornheiser decided to take an informal poll of typical fans to see if they thought the ball was fair or foul. According to his research, boxer Carl "The Truth" Williams thought it was fair, while basketball player Walter "The Truth" Berry thought it was foul. Donald Trump simply wanted to buy the foul pole and rename it "Ump de Trump."

Phillies manager Nick Leyva also had sizable problems with the men in blue. After criticizing NL umpire John McSherry, my old roommate, for his weight, Leyva apologized, saying, "I do owe John an apology. It was said out of frustration. He hasn't hurt us on a call when he's been out of position. And if he's in position, there's no reason for us to even talk about it [his weight]...I made a mistake. I feel like dirt."

Not low enough, Nick, sorry.

In Baltimore, as I've mentioned, Frank Robinson threatened to quit as Orioles manager because, he said, umpires were treating him unfairly. Now why, why, why couldn't my old friend Earl Weaver have made that offer? "All I'm asking is to be able to do my job without being harassed, without being threatened, without being lied to," Robinson said. "All I want to do is be treated like other managers when I have something to say."

Robinson's problems started when my old friend Richie Garcia ejected him for arguing over an interference call. Richie said that Frank was just arguing to try to shake up his team. "It's an old Earl Weaver tactic," he said. "Earl would have probably given him an A-plus."

"The whole thing is totally ridiculous," Marty Springstead said. "How can he say we single anyone out when he has a five-and-a-half-game lead?"

And Kenny Kaiser summed it up correctly, pointing out, "If we didn't have it in for Earl, why would we have it in for Frank? Frank's a small-time complainer compared to Earl."

And believe me, it's tough to be smaller than Earl.

The Most Unusual Ejection of the Year Award goes to...now really, who else would it be? Right, my friend, the great veteran umpire Kenny Kaiser, who actually ejected Terry Francona after he was intentionally walked. I can assure you, Francona was not arguing over a call. This particular confrontation went back to a game played almost a month earlier, in which Kaiser had ruled that a line drive hit by Francona had been caught, not trapped. Then, about a week before this intentional-walk argument took place, Kaiser had been hit in the throat by a foul tip that almost killed him. So, while the pitcher was throwing four wide pitches, Francona told Kaiser, "See, stuff like that wouldn't happen to you if you didn't make bad calls." Naturally, Kaiser responded politely; it's even possible he suggested some anatomical impossibilities. That started a real argument, which ended in Francona's ejection.

For Kenny, it was as if the umpire's worst nightmare had come true. "I'm dying," he said, "and he's screaming at me about a play I don't even remember."

Maybe the only manager to emerge from a confrontation with an umpire in 1989 at least partially satisfied was Don Zimmer. So what if he took a team picked to finish at the bottom of its division and won the title? The really impossible thing he did was win an argument with an umpire. In the fourth inning of a game against the Reds, the Cubs' Ryne Sandberg was on second base and Damon Berryhill was the batter. Berryhill hit a grounder toward third. Cincinnati third baseman Chris Sabo dived for it, and missed, but after the ball went past him, it hit Sandberg on the leg. Instinctively, umpire Bob Engel called Sandberg out for interference, citing the rule that states a runner is out when hit by a batted ball. Zimmer stormed out of the dugout and started screaming at Engel, reminding him that the rule says that the runner is not out if the ball hits him after passing a fielder. Engel compromised: he upheld Zimmer's protest, but threw him out of the game anyway. That proved that everybody's parents were right all along—it's not what you say, but how you say it. Or, in this case, how you scream it two inches from the umpire's face. At least Zimmer got some satisfaction. "After forty-one years in this game," he said proudly, "I finally heard an umpire say I was right—but I still got robbed."

Umpiring history was made in 1989 when Mark and John Hirschbeck became the first brothers to umpire in the big leagues at the same time. Although they're working in different leagues, they're hoping to work together in a World Series one day. When their father was asked if that would create a dilemma for him, because he wouldn't know which league to root for, he shook his head and said, "No problem. I used to be a Yankee fan. Now I'm an umpire fan. I just root for the umpires."

That's one.

Mets manager Davey Johnson was thinking about umpires when he started taking voice lessons from singer Julius La Rosa. Johnson explained that his voice just didn't carry enough when he was in a discussion with an umpire, so he wanted to strengthen his stomach muscles.

Of course, if that's all it took to win an argument, Enrico Caruso would have been a great manager.

Managers and players are willing to blame umpires for everything that goes wrong—even rain. Here's a confession: umpires don't really control the weather. All right, except indoors. But the truth is that umpires don't know when it's going to stop raining any more than, say, weathermen do. So when a game is being delayed because of rain, the umpires call the local weather station, which is usually located at the nearest airport, to get a current forecast. One day, that caused pitcher Ricky Horton to complain during a rain delay, "The umpires said they heard reports that the rain would stop in fifteen minutes. That was about an hour ago. They must have called the wrong airport. That's always been one of my favorite expressions, 'It's not raining at the airport.' As if we're supposed to play on Runway 2."

Possibly the best suggestion of 1989 was made by third baseman Tom Brookens. After third base umpire Rick Reed had called a ball that landed at least five feet foul a home run, explaining that it passed over the top of the foul pole in fair territory, Brookens said to him, "You know, that really was too close to call. Let's play it over."

A Big Hand for the Pitcher

The Nicest Story of 1989 is that of left-handed pitcher Jim Abbott. Abbott, who was born without a right hand, was the hero of the United States gold-medal winning team in the '88 Olympics, and in '89 became only the fifteenth player since the inception of the big league draft to jump directly from amateur baseball to the big leagues. Abbott earned the fifth spot on the California Angels' staff in spring training. In addition to the normal pressure faced by rookies, the twenty-one-year-old constantly had to answer questions about being born without a right hand; questions like, "Are you the only one in your family with a birth defect?" When one reporter asked him how he'd react to a line drive hit right back at him, he replied, "I'll do what everybody else does. I'll duck."

After he'd made his spring training debut, a writer asked him if he would have fielded a potential double-play bouncer if he'd had two hands. "If I had two hands," Abbott answered patiently, "I might have bobbled it."

In his first regular-season appearance, Abbott was beaten by the Mariners. He made his first error on a hard ground ball hit right back at him: he picked it up and threw it away.

By the end of the '89 season Abbott had convinced all doubters that he could pitch, and win, in the major leagues, winning 12 games against 12 losses. His roughest period came in August, when he was hit hard in several consecutive starts. Finally he faced the Red Sox in Fenway Park, probably the toughest park in the majors for a left-hander to win in. The day before, the Red Sox had beaten California 13–5 and 8–4 in a double-header, but Abbott threw a masterful four-hit shutout to beat them. Pitching coach Marcel Lachemann said Abbott pitched well because all the coaches on the bench had finally left him alone, but Jim Abbott had another explanation: "I think the Red Sox just got tired from scoring so many runs."

Out of Their Major League

Baseball is played in a lot of other leagues besides the majors and minors. Probably the best known of all the other leagues is the Little League. Once, as shortstop Jay Bell said, "They used to say that baseball players were a bunch of grown men playing a kid's game. That's not how it is now. Now the Little Leaguers are a bunch of kids playing a man's game."

The 1989 Little League World Series was won by Trumbull, Connecticut, who beat Taiwan to become the first American team in six seasons to win the championship. But the biggest story of the Series was the first appearance of a girl on an American team. Victoria Brucker not only played for the Western regional champions, San Pedro, California; she was their leading home run hitter. "They think she's a girl," one of her teammates explained, "so they just pitch fastballs and she hits them out."

Which sort of gives credibility to a theory of mine: in the 1990s, in addition to talking about women's rights, we'll be talking about women right fielders.

The Little League winner of the Like Father, Like Son Award is Tommy Edward John III, son of pitching star Tommy John. Tommy II was known for tantalizing batters with the pitches he threw at three different speeds: slow, slower, and parked. "I can throw pretty hard," Tommy John III admitted, "but I throw slow balls to stupid kids who swing at everything."

In college baseball, Wichita State upset the heavily favored University of Texas to win its first NCAA baseball championship. But again, in college, the big news of the year was made by Julie Croteau of St. Mary's College of Maryland, who became the first woman to play in an official NCAA baseball game. Croteau, a first baseman, handled six chances without an error and grounded out three times in her debut against Spring Garden College. "I thought she was one of their better players," Spring Garden's coach said after the game, "especially at bat. She didn't get any hits, but she looked good."

In real international league play, the first Russian amateur baseball team to visit the United States played a ten-game tour. They lost their first game to the Naval Academy, 21–2. They lost their second game to George Washington, 20–1. Obviously, they were improving. Baseball is a brand-new game in Russia, even though *Pravda* claims the Russians invented it. They picked up the fundamentals slowly; for example, during infield practice the third baseman wore all the catcher's protective gear.

Pirates coach Rich Donnelly claimed that he'd been told by a friend on the Russian team that the Russians had been warned that if they didn't play well they would be sent to Siberia when they returned. "He didn't mind, though," Donnelly explained. "He said he always wanted to play winter ball."

And finally, the Senior Professional Baseball Association, a hardball league for players over thirty-five years old, began play in Florida in 1989. "This is not for guys who have trouble fitting into a uniform," former Dodgers catcher Steve Yeager said. "And so what if some of us have lost a step? I wasn't that fast to begin with."

When Whitey Herzog was asked if he intended to play

in the league, he laughed, then said, "Why? I was no good in my prime."

When the league finally did begin play, the most serious problem they faced was the high number of minor injuries, like pulled muscles. Graig Nettles probably summed up the quality of play in the league when he pointed out, "We had what we called the 'hit and limp' sign."

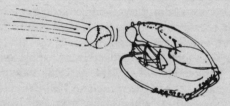

Trade Wins—and Losses

Trades were much rougher to make than ever before in 1989 because so many players had long-term contracts, were about to become free agents and wouldn't sign a new contract, were being paid too much in their old contract, or had a no-trade clause in their contract. So general managers made whatever deals they could. For example, the Phillies sent pitcher Larry McWilliams to Kansas City in exchange for "possible future considerations." Phillies general manager Lee Thomas explained, "It was the best deal I could make."

Similarly, the Blue Jays traded pitcher Jeff Musselman to the Mets for a player to be named later. Toronto pitcher Mike Flanagan wondered, "Where are they going to find a player without a name? Are they going to find a ten-minute-old baby whose parents haven't decided on a name? And, let's be honest, how much could a player like that really help us?"

As usual, though, the Yankees still managed to make more than their share of deals. They had so many players coming and going that Don Mattingly said after Mike Pagliarulo was traded to San Diego, "I saw in the papers a few days ago that if we don't start playing well, we're going to see some new faces around here. We don't have many old faces."

When Yankee pitcher John Candelaria claimed he was thinking about retiring and moving to Paris if the Yankees didn't give him a two-year contract extension, the team did the next best thing: it traded him to Montreal, where the people speak French.

Actually, a lot of players were very happy to be traded to the Yankees. "I'm a 100 percent Yankee," Jesse Barfield said after being traded to New York from Toronto. "I knew that when I didn't have to listen to two national anthems."

Pitcher Greg Cadaret, who came to the Yankees from Oakland, said, "My wife gets a kick out of seeing how cars get stripped when we drive home. New York is the only city in the world where you have a flat tire and the car's totaled."

Obviously, it takes a player a little time to adjust to playing with a new team. When Andy Van Slyke played for the Cardinals he owned a house in St. Louis, but now, when the Pirates visit St. Louis, he stays with the team in a hotel. "For me, the biggest difference between living here and visiting here is that you can't go downstairs for coffee. They won't let you in the restaurant in your underwear."

The Worst Trade of the Year Award goes to the Pittsburgh Pirates who sent Mike Dunne, a 13-game winner in '87, and two top minor league prospects to Seattle for shortstop Rey Quinones and a minor league pitcher. Three months after making the deal the Pirates gave

Quinones—who was hitting .209 and fielding erratically—his release. Of course, Pirates manager Jim Leyland had a good explanation for the deal. "We never would have made the trade if we didn't think he could play."

The Worst Non-Trade of the Year Award is shared by the Pirates and Astros. The two teams worked out a deal sending Pittsburgh's Glenn Wilson to Houston for Alan Ashby. Ashby has been in the big leagues ten years, five with the same team, which gave him the right to veto the deal. And when the Pirates refused to renegotiate his $550,000 salary, he did. A few days later, Houston released him. And Pittsburgh, who then could have signed him as a free agent, decided they didn't want him. "He didn't want to play here," Leyland said, then added, "This ain't purgatory here."

Because it's so tough to complete a major deal, most trades really don't improve either team. For example, in the off-season, the Giants traded Mike Aldrete to Montreal for Tracy Jones. When the two teams met for the first time, in May, Jones was hitting .098, and Aldrete was hitting .170. Both players got base hits in their first at bats—and then were caught stealing.

And even after the Phillies had almost totally revamped their ball club with deals that brought in young players, general manager Lee Thomas admitted, "We're still going to take our lumps."

The Serious World

After the Giants had neatly disposed of the Cubs in the National League playoffs, and the A's had dispatched the Blue Jays, San Francisco and Oakland prepared for the Bay Bridge World Series. "I always felt this is what I wanted most," Giants general manager Al Rosen said as he made one of the worst predictions in sports history. "The Giants and the A's. There's nobody who lives in this area who won't be talking about the World Series for the next ten days."

Oakland easily won the first two games of the Series by combining great hitting with outstanding pitching. After the second game Giants manager Roger Craig was asked how he intended to stop Oakland's attack. "I think I'll move my outfielders back," he said. "I'll have 'em play behind the fences."

And then he was asked what he could teach his batters about hitting the split-fingered fastball, a pitch he practically invented, which was being thrown by almost every pitcher on the A's staff. "I taught our team how to throw it," Craig said somewhat sadly; "I didn't teach them how to hit it."

Before the third game was played, there was some fear that the notorious freezing winds that normally sweep through Candlestick Park after sundown would affect the games. Instead, the weather was warm and beautiful, causing Giants batting coach Dusty Baker to suggest,

"This is probably the time of year they sold the Giants this property."

But suddenly, just as broadcasters Al Michaels and Tim McCarver were welcoming viewers to the third game of the Series, a powerful earthquake struck the Bay Area. After confirming the broadcast could still be heard, Michaels said, "Well, folks, that's the greatest opening in the history of television."

Will Clark, suffering from the flu, was jogging in the outfield when the quake hit. "I knew I was sick, but I didn't think I was that sick. I had to stop running. The ground was moving quicker than I was."

Because of the severity of the quake, there was some doubt that the Series would continue. Many people questioned whether it was safe to play at Candlestick. "We've been trying to get rid of this ball park for a while now," Giants owner Bob Lurie said, "but I really don't think this is the way to do it."

Finally, Commissioner Vincent decided that after a twelve-day lay-off, the Series would be resumed. Roger Craig was asked if he would permit his family to attend the games. "If they want to go," he said. "From what I hear, the stadium's been checked out and it's perfectly safe. So I'm not afraid of it, really.

"But I am going to manage from second base."

In fact, it wouldn't have mattered where he managed from. The Oakland A's were simply too strong for the Giants and won the 1989 Series in four straight games. "The only thing the Giants didn't have," Jose Canseco said after the final game, "was what we have."

The End of the Diamond

The last season of the 1980s was also the last season for a lot of familiar names—unless they sign with the Senior League. A year after he was released by the Minnesota Twins, Steve Carlton announced he was finished as a player—but he refused to use the word "retired," instead saying, "I've decided I would no longer be active as a player." However, Carlton admitted that he still had hope that he might be able to continue his pitching career in Japan. "I like to pitch anywhere," he said. "I liked Cleveland."

His former Phillies teammate Mike Schmidt retired in mid-season. With tears flowing from his eyes, Schmidt told reporters, "You may not be able to tell, but this is a joyous time for me...I've had a handful of times nobody had. My flame just went out."

After watching Schmidt announce his retirement, several Pirate players were talking about how they'd like to end their careers. "When my time comes," Andy Van Slyke said, "I'd like to go up in a hot-air balloon and float away right from center field."

After forty-two seasons in uniform, Houston Astros coach Yogi Berra announced his retirement at the end of the season. "I figured after forty-two years it was time to try something else," he said.

Nineteen eighty-nine looked as if it might be the last season for one-time star reliever Goose Gossage, who was released by the Cubs, Giants, and Yankees. After being released by the Cubs, the Goose was philosophical about his future. "I'll go fishing," he said. "The most important thing in my life is my family. My boys are starting to play baseball now. I'll go over and boo them."

While Schmidt said what he would miss about the game was the relationships he had with his teammates, the Red Sox' great reliever Bob Stanley said upon leaving Yankee Stadium for the final time in his career, "That's the last time I'll ever hear Frank Sinatra singing, 'New York, New York.'"

Like Carlton, Tommy John refused to announce his retirement, hoping some team might give him a chance to pitch. He felt he could still win in the big leagues, claiming, "My fastball is even better than it was in spring training."

Tim Flannery, never a star, but a solid major leaguer, retired on his birthday in late September and said with great satisfaction, "How many times can a grunt go out in style?"

And finally, Yankee great Ron Guidry attempted to come back from arm surgery, but after spending two months in the minor leagues, announced his retirement and returned to his home in Lafayette, Louisiana. "I love it here," he said in Louisiana. "Course, there's not as much night life as there is in New York." And, after thinking about it for a moment, he added, "And there's not as much day life, either."

It's About Time

Unlike most people, baseball players tend to measure time in games and seasons. In the language of baseball, there really are only three different time periods: yesterday, today, and tomorrow. And as far as yesterday goes, I think Howard Johnson was absolutely correct when he told his Mets teammates, "Yesterday is over."

Which, of course, leaves today. Today is always the most important day. As John Candelaria said, "A career might end on one pitch. Why worry about tomorrow when it's today?"

Randy Velarde agreed, saying, "I can't worry about next year when today is so important."

Maybe the Blue Jays general manager, Pat Gillick, summed it up best when he pointed out, "I think our players realize they have to play for today and worry about tomorrow, tomorrow." Of course, if you wait for tomorrow to worry about tomorrow, then tomorrow really is another day.

I guess Don Zimmer summed it up best, saying flatly, "I don't care about tomorrow."

And that was certainly agreeable to John Franco, who said after watching the Giants trade for a player they needed for the pennant race, "I guess Al Rosen is thinking about today instead of tomorrow."

Of course, Keith Hernandez probably didn't mean it when he said, "Time is running out"; to which Mets coach Sam Perlozzo added, "You can't keep saying to-morrow's another day. Another days are running out."

Tomorrow isn't another day?

But I think the Cubs' Ryne Sandberg probably got it right when he stated flatly, "Nothing is better than the present."

The Last Words

...belong to Lloyd Moseby, who said at the end of the season, "Don't ask me about baseball anymore. It's over, and I'm going home."

We hope you have enjoyed the first annual edition of *Baseball Lite*. As in any annual collection, there are obviously things we missed and changes we intend to make. We'd really like to hear your comments and suggestions, and most important, your contributions to the funny, warm, and odd things that happen on the baseball fields of our lives. So please, if you see, hear, or are even part of an event that you believe belongs in *Baseball Lite*, write to us at:

Ron Luciano's Baseball Lite
P.O. Box 631
Union Station
Endicott, New York 13760

About the Authors

Former major league umpire Ron Luciano is the co-author of five books, including the best-sellers *The Umpire Strikes Back*, and *Strike Two*. A popular TV commentator on baseball, he claims to be entering the eighth year of his two-month miracle diet.

His collaborator, David Fisher, is the author of more than 40 books. He recently worked with George Burns on the best-sellers *Gracie* and *All My Best Friends*, and with Sparky Lyle on the Bantam novel *The Year I Owned the Yankees*. He also created and edited the international best-selling reference book *What's What*.

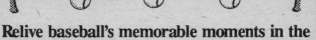